EMBRACE

SHOWING AND SHARING
THE LOVE OF JESUS

EMBRACE

SHOWING AND SHARING
THE LOVE OF JESUS

Kimberly Dunnam Reisman
World Methodist Evangelism

Nashville, TN

Embrace
Showing and Sharing the Love of Jesus

ISBN 13: 978-1-7910-2358-4
ePub ISBN 978-1-7910-2369-0

Cover Illustration by Kerry D. Peeples

21 22 23 24 25 26 27 28 29 30—10 9 8 7 6 5 4 3 2 1
MANUFACTURED IN THE UNITED STATES OF AMERICA

TABLE OF CONTENTS

Introduction 7

Guide For Reading And Weekly Discussion 9

Session One • The Ground On Which We Stand. 11
   Our Foundation: Father ~ Son ~ Holy Spirit 14
   Group Meeting ~ Session One. 23

Session Two • Opening Our Arms 27
   Group Meeting ~ Session Two 45

Session Three • Waiting In The Power Of The Spirit 47
   Group Meeting ~ Session Three. 64

Session Four • Closing Our Arms. 67
   Group Meeting ~ Session Four 81

Session Five • Opening Our Arms Again 83
   Group Meeting ~ Session Five. 93

Session Six • Abundant Life 95
   Group Meeting ~ Session Six. 106

Endnotes 108

INTRODUCTION

SEVERAL YEARS AGO, I attended an art exhibit and recognized an acquaintance from the community. As he introduced me to his wife, he mentioned I was working on my PhD but was unsure of the area. When I responded, "the theology of evangelism," their response was immediate. With perfect timing, they both stepped back with a look of horror on their faces. He was embarrassed that their reaction was so obvious and negative, so he quickly apologized saying, "Evangelism, wow. I never would have thought. You've always struck me as so open-minded and compassionate." As I tried to ease his discomfort, I realized how difficult it would be to convince him that it was possible to be committed to evangelism and at the same time be open-minded and compassionate.

Sadly, this experience is not unique. Over and over, across denominations and both within and outside the church, people respond with hesitation, frustration, misunderstanding, denial, negativity, and even outright hostility when they hear the word *evangelism*. It seems most people, at least in the Western world, do not like talking about evangelism and are even more uncomfortable doing it. At its core, however, evangelism is simply showing and sharing the love of Jesus.[1] *Embrace* helps Christ followers become more comfortable, confident, and competent in doing just that—showing and sharing the love of Jesus.

Embrace offers a new way to think about evangelism. This new way recognizes the need to approach both the gospel and the formation of faith holistically. Through the metaphor of embrace, I believe we can discover a new "stance" or way of being in the world to undergird everything we do in evangelism. Further, the metaphor of embrace points to six values that make up the essence of authentically showing and sharing the love of Jesus: humility, clarity, prayer, integrity, worship, and urgency.

My encounter at the art gallery illustrates that across the world, trust in people who evangelize is very low, and understandings of evangelism are often based on negative images and uncomfortable impressions. This is true both within and outside the church. In this kind of atmosphere, it is crucial to restore evangelism to its proper place of integrity within the community of faith and beyond. It is my hope that picturing evangelism as flowing from a posture of embrace will help to restore the confidence, wholeness, and responsiveness to the power of the Holy Spirit, which undergirds all Christian witness.

I am grateful to Miroslav Volf for the initial metaphor of embrace. Volf is a Croatian theologian. Early in his career, he wrote *Exclusion and Embrace: A Theological Exploration of Identity, Otherness, and Reconciliation.*[2] This book had a profound effect on me and played a large part in my PhD work. Volf uses the metaphor of embrace to discuss reconciliation; however, I believe it is equally important as a way to understand evangelism. Reconciliation and evangelism are different; yet they are bound up in each other. When we share our faith, we become ambassadors for Christ, and engage in the task of reconciling people to him (2 Corinthians 5:18-21). In offering the metaphor of embrace to understand evangelism, I believe I have expanded its power; yet I remain thankful to Volf for providing the guiding idea.

Over the years, World Methodist Evangelism has also influenced my ministry in a significant way. *Embrace* draws upon and expands the work of H. Eddie Fox and George E. Morris in their book, *Faith-Sharing: Dynamic Christian Witnessing by Invitation.*[3] More than twenty years ago, Fox and Morris saw the need to empower people to gracefully share their faith. They used WME as a platform for that ministry. As Executive Director of WME, I am following in their footsteps. In writing *Embrace*, I pray that it will provide both continuity with the past and a fresh vision for the future.

GUIDE FOR READING AND WEEKLY DISCUSSION

EMBRACE PROVIDES A holistic understanding of evangelism to equip Christ followers to share their faith with confidence, competence, and grace. It is divided into six sessions, with a group meeting at the end of each session. Each session contains short sections of reading, followed by questions to help you think about your own experience. Space is provided for you to write down your thoughts and responses. These notes are an excellent way for you to understand and raise questions about what you have read. They will also provide reminders for you during your weekly small group discussion.

The weekly small group meetings are an important part of the *Embrace* experience. This guide provides a general strategy for those group discussions. Specific suggestions are included at the end of each session to facilitate conversation and sharing.

THE *EMBRACE* JOURNEY

During your six weeks together, group meetings will become most meaningful if they reflect the experience of all the participants. Below are suggestions to help with your sharing and conversation.

- *Opening Prayer.* Begin each session with a time of prayer to center the group on the essential value that will be discussed.
- *Insights and Challenges.* Encourage each person to share one new insight and one challenging idea they encountered during the weekly reading.
- *Sharing Together.* This is the core of each session. It should include broad participation and take up the bulk of your time together. As you explore the material together, be sensitive to the needs and experiences of everyone in the group.

- *Act on It.* Each session closes with an opportunity to apply what you have discovered. Share how members of your group are applying what they are learning in their daily lives. Session Two offers a definition of Christian faith. Each week after that session, invite at least one person to share their experience of coming to faith in Jesus Christ.
- *Pray About It.* Group prayer is one of the great blessings of Christian community. There is power in shared prayer. Prayer is one of the essential values of showing and sharing the love of Jesus and it will be a significant aspect of your journey together. Suggestions for your closing prayer time are included at the end of each session.

Register Today

REGISTER YOURSELF AS a leader or group member at www.worldmethodist.org/embrace/. You will receive updates to encourage you on the *Embrace* journey.

For more information about *Embrace* evangelism training and workshops, contact World Methodist Evangelism:

PO Box 8142

Lafayette, IN 47903

worldmethodist.org

info@worldmethodist.org

EMBRACE:

THE GROUND ON WHICH WE STAND

In the beginning God created the heavens and the earth. . . . Then God looked over all he
had made, and he saw that it was very good!
Genesis 1:1, 31 (NLT)
In the beginning the Word already existed. The Word was with God, and the Word was God.
He existed in the beginning with God. God created everything through him,
and nothing was created except through him.
John 1:1-3 (NLT)

SEVERAL YEARS AGO, I was teaching in Seattle, Washington, and went hiking with my husband at Rattlesnake Ledge, just outside the city. It was an energizing hike, and the view at the top was spectacular. As we hiked, the beauty pressed in upon me and one thought kept running through my mind. Creation is never an extra in Christian faith. It is foundational. Christian faith begins with creation and all else moves outward from there.

That idea is not always as obvious as it should be. As Christians, we do not always begin with our Creator God. It is easy to flip things around and begin with ourselves and our redemption. We think of God as the Redeemer who *also* creates, rather than as the Creator who also redeems. Unfortunately, that idea is a mistake that happens when we place *ourselves* at the center of the universe, instead of the one who truly belongs there—God.

God creates, *then* God redeems. Christian faith is deepened and enriched when we get the order right. This is especially true when it comes to sharing our faith. When faith in Jesus Christ is born in us, it is not just faith in Jesus Christ; it is faith in a *Triune God*—Father, Son, and Holy Spirit. Of course, Jesus is vital, but our creeds remind us of the order. We believe in God, the Father, Almighty, Maker of heaven and earth. Starting there widens the scope of redemption and helps us realize it is indeed good news *for all creation.*

As we explore the six values that make up authentic evangelism, *we begin with our Creator God.* That is the ground on which everything rests. Because sharing our faith is influenced by environment and culture, practices may vary. Methods and strategies that bear fruit in one part of the world may be inappropriate in another part of the world. Yet, when the *essence* of sharing faith, those values that lie *beneath* our practices, rest firmly on an understanding of our creating, redeeming, and sustaining God—Father, Son, and Holy Spirit—there will be a consistent "way of being in the world" that colors all our efforts, regardless of where we live or the distinctive aspects of our culture.

To explore this "way of being," it is important to recognize that sin—our need for redemption—is not the *reason* for God's grace. God's grace is part of God's *very nature.* God's grace was alive and active long before sin entered the picture. It was God's grace that brought creation into existence, and it will abound overwhelmingly, long after sin has been eliminated and God's new creation is experienced in all its fullness.

As Christians, we worship a creating, redeeming, sustaining God—Father, Son, and Holy Spirit. Our God redeems not only human beings but also the whole of creation. Paul even tells us that creation is groaning as God continues to work to redeem it (Romans 8:22-23). We worship a creating, redeeming, sustaining God—Father, Son, and Holy Spirit—and our God is working, even

God creates.

God redeems.

Christian faith is deepened and

enriched

when we get

the order right.

now, to eliminate evil and fulfill the justice and peace of the kingdom that began in Jesus. It is this God who creates. It is this God who redeems.

How have you thought of God in the past—as a redeeming God who also creates? Or as a creating God who also redeems? How does this order affect how you approach people outside the church? Make a few notes on your reflections.

God's grace is part of God's *very nature*. God's grace brought creation into existence long before sin entered the picture, and it will abound overwhelmingly, long after sin has been eliminated and God's new creation is experienced in all its fullness.

How might your understanding be deepened by beginning with creation rather than with redemption?

How might you approach faith-sharing differently if you understood the good news to be "for *all* creation"?

OUR FOUNDATION:
FATHER ~ SON ~ HOLY SPIRIT

GOD THE FATHER

One of the first things we notice when we look to the Trinity as our foundation is that sharing our faith begins from a positive place. It begins with the goodness of creation and God's faithfulness to it. It begins with God's desire for creation to be whole. Human beings desperately need redemption, but God did not create simply so that God could redeem. God redeems out of faithfulness to the loving relationship that is formed when God freely creates.

Intertwined with this is our understanding that God created our world out of nothing. In creating, God makes new space within Godself. God moves back from God's own boundaries, so to speak, to make room for something completely new and different from God. This new and different thing is creation. God creates this new space so that God can then fill the new space with creation. And then God reaches out to this new creation to form relationship. That is what John Wesley was talking about when he taught about God's "holy love." For Wesley, God's love is not static. It began moving outward from the moment of creation when God freely chose to give God's very self. It continues moving as God "stoops down" to make contact and form relationship.[4]

> Human beings desperately need redemption, but God did not create simply to be able to redeem. God redeems out of faithfulness to the loving relationship that is formed when God freely creates.

This is significant because God's space-making, self-giving activity in creation is not only a central part of the Christian message, it is also the *model* for that message. In the same way God makes room within Godself for creation, we make room within ourselves for other people. And we make new space within ourselves especially for those who do not yet know Jesus Christ or who are currently outside the boundaries of our faith communities.

In thinking about God, the Father, write down any new insights that you received that you had not thought of before.

How might your approach to showing and sharing the love of Jesus change if you thought of it as flowing from God's faithfulness?

In the same way God makes room within Godself for creation, we make room within ourselves for other people, especially those who do not yet know Jesus Christ or who are currently outside the boundaries of our faith communities.

GOD THE SON

Our foundation begins with God's self-giving in creation and extends to God's self-giving in Jesus Christ. At the heart of our faith is the belief that God became human in Jesus, and in Jesus, the

Redemption is not the process of being redeemed from creation. Redemption is the redeeming of all creation. Through Jesus Christ, the entire physical universe, including human beings, is perfected and restored to its intended integrity and wholenes

The life and death of Jesus Christ reveal a crucial pattern for evangelism: radical obedience to God and selfless love toward other people.

redemption of all creation has begun. This is important because it highlights God's faithfulness, not just to humanity but also to the entire physical universe. *The destiny of the whole world is tied up in Jesus Christ.* Thus, redemption is not the process of being redeemed *from* creation. Creation is not something that needs to be escaped from or destroyed for a new creation to come into existence. When God created the universe, God called it very good. Therefore, redemption is the redeeming *of* creation, where *all* of creation (not only human beings) is perfected and restored. Full redemption is when God's holy love is in all and over all.

God's self-giving in Jesus Christ becomes an even clearer model for sharing our faith when we recognize the two themes of the cross. As our crucified Lord, Jesus stands in solidarity with all who have suffered. At the same time, Jesus offers atonement to all who have sinned and fallen short. In other words, God's self-donation is for both the oppressed and the oppressor, the perpetrator and the victim.[5] It is impossible to understand the fullness of God's self-giving love without both aspects. It is impossible as well to understand the holistic nature of showing and sharing the love of Jesus without these twin themes. Christ's self-giving love overcomes human hatred and also creates space within Christ to receive estranged humanity. These two dimensions, the giving of self and the receiving of another, are a basic part of God's nature and therefore form the foundation for sharing our faith.[6]

The life and death of Jesus Christ reveal a crucial pattern for us: radical obedience to God and selfless love toward other people. As we explore the essential values of showing and sharing the love of Jesus, we will not discover a mandate to perform certain deeds or learn particular doctrines. We will discover a pattern laid out for us in the life and death of Jesus.[7]

Reflect on what you have read about God's self-donation in Jesus Christ. How does that fit into your current understanding?

Do you think of evangelism more as verbal communication of a set of doctrines, or as an integrated lifestyle of self-giving witness? Why?

What are some examples of both that you have seen practiced well? What are some examples of both that you have seen practiced poorly?

GOD THE HOLY SPIRIT

The underlying force of God's kingdom is the power of the Holy Spirit of God. God's Holy Spirit was present at creation and continues to sustain it in life. It was God's Holy Spirit who empowered Jesus and descended on his followers at Pentecost. It is only through the power of the Holy Spirit that we are able to continue Jesus' mission of self-sacrificing love in the world. Without Holy Spirit power, we lack the boldness and courage necessary to live in this "in between" time when God's kingdom has not yet fully come on earth as it is in heaven.

One of the most wonderful things about Christian faith is that our Creator God—the one who at times can seem larger than our ability to understand—is also an ever-present, enabling God, a God who at other times seems closer to us than our breath.[8] This enabling God is the Holy Spirit, the one who inspires our prophetic witness to Jesus Christ (Luke/Acts), and resides within each of us (John).

The Holy Spirit is focused in Jesus Christ and concentrated in those who follow him but is not contained only within the church. Instead, the Holy Spirit is present, active, and involved with *all* of creation in a life-giving way (Psalm 139:7; 2 Corinthians 3:6; Romans 8:1-27).[9] Through the Holy Spirit, God gives Godself away to us. Through the Holy Spirit, God shares our sufferings, joins us in our misery, and binds Godself to us in joy and sorrow. It is the Holy Spirit that conforms us into the image of Christ.

The grace of the indwelling Spirit allows us to participate in the life of God and gives us power. This grace is our saving strength. When we ground faith-sharing in our creating, redeeming, and sustaining God, we open ourselves to being transformed by the Holy Spirit of God. We also open ourselves to becoming channels for that life-changing power in others. In the space created within

Through the Holy Spirit, God shares our sufferings, joins us in our misery, and binds Godself to us in joy and sorrow.

us, and between us and others, the Holy Spirit is invited to transform, not only the other person but us as well.

Because God's kingdom has not yet been made fully known, our experiences of the Holy Spirit are presently incomplete. Yet, these experiences lead to our hope for the future, when God will indeed live completely and fully in God's creation. As we are enlivened by the Spirit, we have hope that everything God created—human beings, nature, all creation—will be able to share in the fullness of God's eternal life. The presence of the Holy Spirit, then, gives our faith-sharing its future focus. We look forward to the future, already begun in Jesus Christ, when God will be all in all.

What new insight did you receive about God's Holy Spirit?

When the Holy Spirit makes us more like Christ, how does that shape our witness?

How might your understanding of evangelism be deepened by a focus on making space for the Holy Spirit in your life?

EMBRACE: A FOUNDATIONAL METAPHOR

Grounded in the Trinity—Father, Son, and Holy Spirit—we can begin to explore the values that make up the essence of authentic faith-sharing. Together these values form our "way of being" in the world as we show and share the love of Jesus. They form the "posture" we take no matter what differences we encounter in culture or place.

I have found that the metaphor of embrace helps us understand this "way of being." Metaphors are valuable because they allow people to grasp meanings that in many ways are deeper and more profound than can be expressed in plain language. They capture the sense of things rather than a literal description. I believe the metaphor of embrace is valuable for understanding faith-sharing, not because it describes a step-by-step practice but because it points to the atmosphere of vulnerability and openness to others that is necessary regardless of our method or strategy. As we move through the remainder of our study, the metaphor of embrace will be the backdrop for each of the values that make up the essence of authentic faith-sharing.

To grasp the metaphor of embrace, we must first understand the motion involved. Embrace is a connected movement with four stages flowing one after the other: opening our arms, waiting, closing our arms, and then opening them again. Without all four elements, embrace is incomplete. We cannot simply open our arms and wait, or embrace will never actually occur. Likewise, if we open our arms, wait, then close our arms but do not open them again, we have turned embrace into an overbearing grip.[10]

During the next several sessions, we will explore each movement of embrace individually. For now, let's take a brief look at all four.

The first stage, opening our arms, is an almost universally understood sign of welcoming. Our stance is one of humble openness. When we open our arms, we signal that we have made space and at the same time are reaching out.

> Metaphors are valuable because they allow people to grasp meanings that in many ways are deeper and more profound than can be expressed in plain language.

> *Embrace:* Opening our arms. Waiting. Closing our arms. Opening our arms again.

Waiting, the second stage of embrace, can be difficult but is very important. Open arms may initiate movement toward another, but it is not a movement that invades or forces a response. Rather, we wait for the other person to open their arms, and in our waiting, we create space for the Holy Spirit to work within us, and between us and the other person.

The third step toward a full embrace is closing the arms. This is the essence of embrace, but it is impossible without reciprocity—both people must act. As we move through our time together, it will be important to remember that "it takes *two* pairs of arms for *one* embrace."[11]

Finally, we have the last stage of embrace, opening our arms again. An embrace does not create one welded body out of two. It is only complete when our arms open once more. This final opening points to the circular nature of embrace as the open arms of the final stage signal our readiness for the next embrace.

What is your initial response to the metaphor of embrace? How does it resonate with you? Make a few notes.

Grounding our understanding of faith-sharing in the Trinity and picturing it through the metaphor of embrace opens us to an integrated, holistic, and communal vision of salvation. In this view of salvation, all created things will be given the opportunity to participate in God's new creation. Frequently, evangelistic practices are very human-focused and, at times, emphasize a negative message. We sometimes proclaim the power of sin rather than the forgiveness of sin. Or we reduce redemption to only an individualistic, privatized experience. Looking to the Trinity as our foundation emphasizes that salvation is a whole-creation project, extending far beyond an interior, human one.

When God freely made space within Godself for creation, God freely limited God's own power. By limiting God's own power, God created space for humans to genuinely express their free will in response to God's grace. In similar fashion, part of showing and sharing the love of Jesus is the act of limiting our power to create space for other people to freely choose to engage us. It also includes recognizing that in the cross, God has taken into Godself even the experiences of suffering and evil, so nothing and no one are beyond God's inexhaustible love and life-changing power.

Therefore, a stance of embrace as a foundation for sharing faith acknowledges the need for discernment but not for final judgment. Final judgment is for God alone. Further, our efforts gain integrity when we remain keenly aware of prevenient grace. We must always remember that goodness, kindness, holiness, grace, divine presence, creating power, and even salvation itself are present before we ever arrive in a particular situation.[12] Nothing and no one is to be denied the opportunity to participate in God's loving, redemptive relationship with creation.

As we move into our study, let us keep before us the image of the father whose son took all he had and journeyed to a distant land, only to lose himself there. As that father opened his arms to welcome his returning son, so we open our arms to receive people into fellowship with Christ, with us, and with the church.

PRAY ABOUT IT

As you come into God's presence, focus on the ways in which you are currently engaging those outside your community of faith. How important has it been to engage those who may not yet be in a relationship with Christ? Open yourself to the ways in which God might use this study to shape and strengthen your attitude and approach to sharing your faith and reaching out to others on behalf of Jesus Christ.

ACT ON IT

You have absorbed a great deal of information during this session. What was the most important new insight you received? How can you act on that new insight?

GROUP MEETING ~ **SESSION ONE**

OVER THE NEXT six sessions, you will receive the most meaning from your weekly time together if you are able to be sensitive to what is happening in the lives of others in the group. It will be important to encourage all to share their experience. Ideas are important, and we benefit when we wrestle with new ideas as well as with ideas with which we disagree. And yet, the purpose of the group meeting is not to debate ideas. People rather than ideas are at the heart of any discussion of faith-sharing. Thus, the emphasis should be on experiences, feelings, and meaning that arise in response to the ideas you encounter.

OPENING PRAYER
INSIGHTS AND CHALLENGES

Review the notes you made of your reflections during the week.

What new insight did you gain?

What challenge did you encounter?

Invite each person to share an insight and a challenge encountered in the material.

SHARING TOGETHER

1. Spend a few minutes discussing the idea that our understanding of faith-sharing is deepened by beginning with our Creator God who redeems rather than with a redeeming God who also creates. How does that understanding affect how we relate to those beyond the church?
2. Share reflections on the idea of making space as a way to understand God's work in creation. How do we model that as we show and share the love of Jesus?

3. Discuss the idea that God redeems out of faithfulness to the relationship God established with creation. How does that impact our understanding of Jesus?

4. Reflect on the concept of God's sacrifice in Jesus for both perpetrators and victims. Share thoughts on how that affects our understanding of sharing our faith.

5. Spend some time reflecting on how the Holy Spirit shapes our witness.

6. Close your time of sharing with initial reactions to the metaphor of embrace. What resonated most with the group? Why?

ACT ON IT

Invite persons to share how they plan to act on the new insight they gained this week.

PRAY ABOUT IT

Prayer is empowering. Verbalizing thoughts and feelings to God in the presence of fellow believers is also a powerful bonding experience as we journey together in faith. Everyone needs to feel comfortable during times of communal prayer, and silent prayer is as vital as prayers spoken aloud.

I offer the following suggestions to guide your time of prayer; however, they are only suggestions. What happens in your time together—the mood, the needs expressed, the timing—should determine the direction of your group prayer time. Here are some possibilities for your closing period.

1. Invite the group to spend a few minutes in silence, reflecting on each person in the group and what they have shared. Offer a silent sentence prayer of petition or thanksgiving for that person.

2. Invite two or three people to offer a brief, spontaneous prayer, thanking God for the group and for the opportunity to share with others in this learning experience.

3. Close your time by praying aloud together the prayer attributed to Saint Francis:

Lord, make me an instrument of your peace;
  where there is hatred, let me sow love;
  where there is injury, pardon;
  where there is doubt, faith;
  where there is despair, hope;
  where there is darkness, light;
  and where there is sadness, joy.

O Divine Master, grant that I may not so much seek
   to be consoled as to console;
   to be understood as to understand;
   to be loved as to love;
   for it is in giving that we receive;
   it is in pardoning that we are pardoned;
   and it is in dying that we are born to eternal life. Amen.

EMBRACE:

OPENING OUR ARMS

ESSENTIAL VALUES:

HUMILITY

CLARITY

HUMILITY

The LORD had said to Abram, "Leave your native country, your relatives,
and your father's family, and go to the land that I will show you. I will make you into a great
nation. I will bless you and make you famous, and you will be a blessing to others. I will bless
those who bless you and curse those who treat you with contempt.
All the families on earth will be blessed through you."
Genesis 12:1-3 (NLT)

Humility: freedom from pride or arrogance; the quality or state of not thinking you are better than other people.

We must have the humility to see the world as it is, not as we would like it to be or think it should be.

We become most fully who we are not when we reach independence but when we understand our *interdependence* and recognize that we are both separate and connected to those around us.

WHEN WE THINK about evangelism, we usually assume that there are people and groups outside the community of Christian believers who are to be engaged in such a way as to bring them into that community. In other words, we evangelize so that outsiders might be transformed into insiders.

This sense of insiders and outsiders is not negative in itself. However, because human nature is fallen, we are often drawn toward people who are like us, and we can be wary of differences. This wariness can lead to tension around the relationship between those within the community of faith and those not yet a part of it. The relationship can sometimes become more confrontational or even adversarial as we begin to think in terms of "us" and "them."

In light of the universal human leaning toward us/them thinking, humility is one of the most important values of authentically sharing our faith. We must have the humility to see the world as it is, not as we would like it to be or think it should be.

SEEING THE WORLD AS IT IS

To grasp the depth of the humility that is necessary to show and share the love of Jesus, it is helpful to explore human identity and the nature of sin. These are vast subjects, but there are a few basic things that are important for our understanding.

From the very beginning, God's creative process has been a practice of separating and joining. God separates the light from the darkness to create day and night. God joins all the waters together into one place to create dry land. In like fashion, our identities are formed as we navigate a process of separating and joining. We become most fully who we are not when we reach independence but when we understand our *interdependence.* We become most fully ourselves when we recognize that we are both separate and connected to those around us. As Miroslav Volf has said, "The boundaries that mark our identities are both barriers *and* bridges."[13]

How have you experienced independence and interdependence, or separation and connectedness, as you have matured in life and faith?

Though God desires us to discover our interdependence, the reality of human sin makes us more inclined to focus on our independence. If we think of God's creative process as separating and joining, there is a meaningful sense in which sin disconnects what God has bound together and unites what God has separated. It disrupts God's pattern of interdependence, making us estranged from one another and from God.[14]

As Christians, we believe that through Abraham *all* of humanity will receive God's blessings. This belief is reflected in the Scripture passage that began this session. God promises that through Abraham, all the families of the earth will be blessed. In keeping this promise, God plans to redeem the overarching situation of estrangement that affects every human being.[15]

Remembering God's promise to redeem all the families of the earth, as well as the ideas about identity and sin, helps us cultivate humility. An additional help is to remember Jesus' remarkable practice of both renaming and remaking. Jesus *renamed* people and things that had been falsely labeled unclean. In this way, he reconnected people and things that sin had wrongly separated (Mark 7:14-23). Jesus also *remade* people and things. He tore down barriers created by wrongdoing by taking truly unclean things and making them clean through forgiveness, spiritual transformation, and healing (Mark 2:15-17; 5:1-20).[16]

God plans to redeem the overarching situation of estrangement that affects *all* human beings.

How have you experienced Jesus' renaming and remaking in your spiritual life?

How might you be a channel for God's renaming and remaking in the lives of others?

Humility is rooted in a constant awareness of the reality of sin and is deeply mindful of the brokenness and woundedness that mark every human life.

The humility that lies at the heart of all faith-sharing is rooted in a constant awareness of the reality of sin in our world. We recognize the brokenness and woundedness that mark human life. We confess that we are no more immune to that brokenness than anyone else, whether within or outside the church. We acknowledge we are unable to redeem our situation of estrangement. We admit we are unable to rename or remake ourselves.

This humility undergirds our way of being in the world and is vividly illustrated in the metaphor of embrace, particularly the first stage—open arms. When we open our arms to initiate embrace, we convey four significant messages.[17] First, our open arms indicate a desire for the other. They signal that "I want you to be part of who I am and I want to be part of you." Open arms point to the deeper truth that a void exists because of the absence of the other.

Open arms also signify that we have made space within ourselves for another. Interestingly, they convey two motions at the same time: we have moved out of ourselves toward the other, and at the same time we have withdrawn from our own boundaries to create new space. In other words, at the same time we are making room within ourselves, we are also journeying toward the other. Similarly, open arms indicate that a gap has opened within our boundaries that will allow the other person to enter. We can desire the other; we can create new space by withdrawing from our own boundaries. If our boundaries are not passable, however, embrace will be impossible.

Lastly, open arms are an invitation. Here is an example. My husband and I have dear friends in our community. There is an understanding between us that our doors are open for each other. Because of this standing invitation, there is no need for either of us to knock. We simply shout, "We're here!" and come on in. Open arms extend such an invitation—yet not only an invitation. They also knock softly on the other's door. In the same way that they both signal a creation of space and a moving out, opening our arms also signals an invitation to come in and a desire to enter the space of the other.

The messages of open arms are important for sharing our faith and the humility that is essential to it. Open arms point to the void created by the absence of some from the divinely promised "one family" of Abraham. They indicate that the boundaries surrounding the one family of Abraham have been made passable and that there is an invitation to shared life, which flows in two directions.

Significantly, open arms convey our humility in the face of human sin. They indicate that though we recognize the estrangement that marks the human condition, we would rather reach out than continue that estrangement. When we open our arms even though the world is not as we would like it to be, we show others that we recognize there is a shared brokenness in being human.

Finally, open arms signify our awareness that the inward making of space and the outward reaching toward another reflect the activity of our Triune God in creation, in its continued care and

> We make room within ourselves, and at the same time journey toward the other. We open a gap within our boundaries to allow them to enter.

> We recognize the estrangement that marks the human condition, but we would rather reach out than continue that estrangement.

sustenance, and in the overarching history of humanity. In pointing to the stance we are to take in relation to those outside the church, open arms reflect the stance of our Triune God toward all of creation.

How have you experienced God's open arms amidst your own brokenness?

Reflect on that experience. Was there a person or persons whom God used in that encounter? What was it about that person or persons that enabled God to use them in that way?

CLARITY

For God, who said, "Let there be light in the darkness," has made this light shine in our hearts
so we could know the glory of God that is seen in the face of Jesus Christ.
2 Corinthians 4:6 (NLT)

Christ is the visible image of the invisible God.
He existed before anything was created and is supreme over all creation,
for through him God created everything in the heavenly realms and on earth . . .
and he holds all creation together. . . .
For God in all his fullness was pleased to live in Christ, and through him God reconciled
everything to himself. He made peace with everything in heaven and on earth
by means of Christ's blood on the cross.
Colossians 1:15-17, 19-20 (NLT)

A common challenge in cultivating a sense of humility is to avoid mistaking it for timidity or faintheartedness. Humility reflects how we see ourselves in relation to others. We recognize that sin infects us all and that every human being, including ourselves, is wounded by its affects. This recognition holds any tendency toward arrogance in check. Timidity and faintheartedness, on the other hand, relate to a deeper, personal understanding of ourselves. This understanding is not connected to our relation to others, but instead is a personal sense of ourselves that can be seen in an inner lack of confidence, determination, or boldness. This is an important distinction when we begin to think of the second essential value of authentic faith-sharing: clarity.

Cultivating an attitude of humility does not mean that we sacrifice confidence, determination, or boldness. Rather, it involves becoming genuinely in touch with our experience of faith and the way that it has impacted our lives. It demands that we be able to share our faith, not as people who have all the answers or who sit in judgment of those who live differently, but as people who have both a deep sense of clarity about what our faith entails and a willingness to engage others with confidence and grace.

Reflect on the distinction between humility and timidity and faintheartedness. How have you experienced that distinction in your own life or witnessed it in the lives of others?

Clarity: the quality or state of being clear; the quality of being understood, expressed, or remembered in a very exact way

Humility demands that we share our faith, not as people who have all the answers or who sit in judgment of those who live differently, but as people who have a deep sense of clarity about what our faith entails and a willingness to engage others with confidence and grace.

The need to be in touch with our experience of faith points to the importance of clarity for authentically showing and sharing the love of Jesus. Clarity is about understanding the nature of Christian faith, both the basic tenets of faith and our experience of it. It is about deliberately attending to the way in which our experience—our story—intersects God's story. Clarity is crucial to authentic faith-sharing because how we understand Christian faith will significantly influence how we share it. Our understanding of how our personal story is interwoven with God's story will impact how we share as well. Regardless of our culture, if we are not clear about the basics of faith, we will be unable to share it authentically. This is especially true in environments where we are surrounded by people who believe differently than we do.

The simple definition of Christian faith found in the *Faith-Sharing New Testament* is helpful in giving us clarity. At its most basic level, Christian faith is a "centered, personal, relational response involving trust and obedience."[18] Much more can be said about Christian faith of course, but this straightforward understanding provides not only a clear outline of the tenets of the faith but also a lens through which we can view our individual experience of it.

CENTERED

The first element of our definition of Christian faith is that it is centered. It has a specific focus. The Scripture passages at the beginning of this session point to that focus: Jesus Christ. Christian faith is centered on "the living God revealed in one Jesus of Nazareth whom we call the Christ, Messiah, the Son of the living God."[19]

We might take this truth for granted, yet it is profoundly important. There is nothing generic about Christian faith. Our world is awash in vague spirituality and emotionally appealing philosophies of life. We may even incorporate practices such as yoga into

Christian faith is a centered, personal, relational response of trust and obedience.

Christian faith is centered on the living God revealed in Jesus of Nazareth whom we call the Christ, the Messiah, the Son of the living God.

our life of discipleship with positive result, but these are not the same as faith itself. Christian faith cannot be reduced to a set of moral principles either, even though world-transforming ethical systems have grown out of our faith. Even our doctrinal propositions, as important as they may be, serve only to anchor us in faith but are not faith itself. Christian faith cannot be painted with a broad brush. It is distinguished by its details, and the central detail on which all else is focused is Jesus Christ.

Reflect on your journey of faith. Where has Jesus Christ appeared in that journey?

PERSONAL

Christian faith is centered, and it is also personal. It is personal because it is fixed on a person—a real human being situated in a real culture at a real time in history. That Jesus was a real person reminds us that Christian faith is grounded in the physical world that God created. Further, Christian faith is centered on a real person who conquered death by rising on the third day. Though mystery abounds, Christian faith is not about a faraway heaven separate from the amazing universe that God created for us to inhabit. Christian faith is about God becoming *human* in Jesus, entering the physical universe and conquering death so that all of creation could be restored fully and completely.

This is connected to our discussion about redemption in Session One. God freely chose to enter the physical universe that God created, which indicates that redemption is not something that takes us *out* of the world. Christian redemption is redemption *of* the whole world, human beings included. That is what heaven is all about. It is not simply a miscellaneous collection of individual souls in an

Christian faith is about God becoming human in Jesus, entering the physical universe to restore it fully and completely.

35

otherworldly realm. Heaven descends to earth. All of creation is delivered from the snare of evil. Everything is redeemed, restored, and made whole once again.

In Revelation 21:2-4 John writes, "I saw the holy city, the new Jerusalem, coming down from God out of heaven like a bride beautifully dressed for her husband. I heard a loud shout from the throne, saying, 'Look, God's home is now among his people! He will live with them, and they will be his people. God himself will be with them. He will wipe every tear from their eyes, and there will be no more death or sorrow or crying or pain. All these things are gone forever'" (NLT). How does the idea that heaven will descend to earth rather than humans escaping to heaven affect your understanding of salvation and redemption?

What impact might such an idea have on how we share our faith?

Christian faith is personal because it is focused on a real person, Jesus Christ, who is alive because of the resurrection. It is also personal because it requires a personal commitment. Because God "respects the sacred right of rejection or acceptance on the part of each human being," our personal commitment is never forced, or one that someone else can make for us.[20] Eddie Fox and George Morris outlined the significance of this aspect of faith:

We can pray that another person might have faith. We can do our best to create an environment in which faith is taught and caught. But we cannot have faith for another person any more than he or she can have faith for us. Faith is so decidedly personal, it demands that each must own that faith for himself or herself.[21]

I understood the personal nature of Christian faith as I was growing up and making faith decisions for myself. However, its significance became clearer to me as I watched my children begin the sometimes rocky process of claiming faith for themselves. That process became especially meaningful in the life of our youngest daughter, Hannah. We claimed Christian faith for each of our three children at their baptism and pledged to do everything in our power to root them firmly in it. And yet, as a young adult, Hannah expressed her struggle to make that faith her own.

It has been said that the longest distance we travel in faith is between the head and the heart. Though Hannah had completed confirmation as a teenager, her faith had not yet taken root in her heart. Thankfully, through the witness and friendship of Christians who were willing to grapple along with her as she questioned and searched, Hannah was able to publicly claim for herself what had previously been done on her behalf. Christian faith is distinctly personal.

Reflect on your experience of claiming Christian faith for yourself. Make some notes about that experience.

RELATIONAL

Christian faith is centered and personal: centered on the person of Jesus, a real human being; personal because each person must have faith for himself or herself. Christian faith is also relational.

Christian faith is relational because it restores our relationship with God, ourselves, others, and creation. Howard Snyder and Joel Scandrett complement our discussion of sin earlier in this session when they describe an "ecology of sin." This ecology involves "alienation from God, internal alienation within each person (alienation from oneself), alienation between humans, and alienation from and within nature." These are the "spiritual, psychological, social, and environmental alienations that afflict the whole human family."[22] Christian faith is the means through which those four alienations are healed.

A fundamental meaning of the English word *salvation* is healing. It comes from the Latin word *salus*, which means health.[23] Christian faith heals our alienation and restores right relationship with God. Paul's word in Ephesians describes this process: "For by grace you have been saved through faith, and this is not your own doing; it is the gift of God" (Ephesians 2:8, NRSV). God takes the initiative, reaching out to us with the gift of grace. Through the power of the Holy Spirit, we are enabled to respond in faith. Estrangement is overcome. We are brought into right relationship with God.

The relational nature of Christian faith extends to our relationship with others. Our alienation from God leads to deep estrangement within the web of human relationships. Faith is the means of healing for those relationships. It rightly relates us to God and rightly relates us to others. We cannot be properly related to God if we are alienated from our neighbor. First John 3:14-16 reminds us that our relationship with God is bound up with our relationship to others, and our relationship to others is bound up with our relationship to God.[24]

> Christian faith restores our relationship with God, self, others, and creation.

> "We know love by this, that he laid down his life for us—and we ought to lay down our lives for one another" (1 John 3:16 NRSV).

38

Finally, Christian faith allows us to establish right relationship with ourselves and with all of creation. It brings new respect for our value as God's beloved children (Romans 8:15-16) and new understanding of our responsibility to be stewards of God's creation. Right relationship with ourselves involves recognizing that though we are beloved by God, we are not at the center of the universe. That is God's place alone. We have been placed amidst creation as stewards. When you are a steward of something it means you do not *own* it, but you are responsible *for* it.

The relational aspect of Christian faith is important because it reminds us that faith is not isolated. If the witness of the birth, life, ministry, death, and resurrection of Jesus shows us anything, it shows that faith is not an isolated endeavor. Relationship is vital. Every story Jesus told, his interaction with other people, his gathering of intimate friends around him—these all point to the significance of relationship.

From our perspective, it appears Jesus often turned relationships upside-down. Yet that perception further highlights the relational change connected to Christian faith. Jesus did not turn relationships upside-down; he transformed them so they would be right-side-up. That is what happens when we come into relationship with God through Jesus Christ. Our relationships are turned right-side-up. We become rightly related to God, others, the world, and ourselves.

How have you experienced the connection between your relationship with God and your relationship with others?

Reflect on how your understanding of yourself has changed because of your faith in Jesus Christ.

How has your relationship with God affected your understanding of yourself as a steward of God's creation?

The overarching relational aspect of Christian faith can be challenging because it is easy to become focused on our interior relationship with God at the expense of the other relationships God seeks to transform. It is not that our personal spiritual life is unimportant. It is crucial. However, when we become too absorbed in our interior, individual experience, we fail to see the all-encompassing, all-creation nature of salvation. When we focus only on individual salvation, our experience of God's redeeming grace is diminished and we miss out on the communal dimension of salvation.

Yet, the good news of the gospel is that God has a plan to save the *whole world*, not simply a collection of individuals. That is why in Paul's letters individual and communal salvation are never separated. As N. T. Wright has written, God's "dealing-with-sin-and-rescuing-people-from-it" (the individual aspect of salvation) and "bringing-Jews-and-Gentiles-together-into-a-single-family" (the communal aspect of salvation) are always bound up together.[25]

Christian faith is relational because we cannot be isolated Christians. Faith happens in the context of community. It is not only individual salvation but communal salvation as well. It is in the context of community that we are rightly related to God, to each other, to the world, and to ourselves.

Do you think of salvation as happening for individuals or communities? Why? What new insights have you gained through the discussion of the whole-creation nature of salvation?

RESPONSE

Faith is centered, it is personal, and it is relational—thus, it requires a response. The fourth element in our definition of Christian faith is that it is a response. Christian faith involves the whole person, not our feelings only. It has been said that "the foundation of faith is not what *we* feel or what *we* have done … it is what *God* feels toward us and what *God* has done on our behalf. [It] is not so much our commitment to God, but God's commitment to us."[26] As we mentioned in the last session, God redeems out of faithfulness to the relationship God created; therefore, God seeks us. God desires from the beginning to be in a relationship of wholeness with us. God's commitment to us comes before all else, and our response is just that—a *response* to God's faithful commitment to us. And it is a response not just of our emotions but of our whole self: body, soul, spirit, intellect.

God seeks us. God desires from the beginning to be in relationship with us. God's plan of redemption "is as broad as the scope of creation."[27] But God does not force or coerce. God's love may actively search for us, always move toward us, but God will not take the last step. That step is ours to take. We must respond for faith to be born in us.

The importance of response is a unique aspect of our Wesleyan understanding of Christian faith. It is a point of contrast with many of our sisters and brothers in other Christian traditions. For those of us in the Wesleyan traditions, God acts *first*, everything is at God's initiation; but our God respects the right of each person to accept or reject God's overture. We must respond. That is how much God loves us—so much that God would never desire to violate us, coerce us, manipulate us, or force us.

Describe your experience of responding to God's grace revealed in Jesus Christ.

TRUST AND OBEDIENCE

"We tend to treasure

what we trust

and trust what we treasure."

"Those who live in the shelter of

the Most High will find rest in the

shadow of the Almighty. This I

declare about the LORD: He alone

is my refuge, my place of safety; he

is my God, and I trust him. For he

will rescue you from every trap and

protect you from deadly disease.

He will cover you with his feathers.

He will shelter you with his wings.

His faithful promises are your armor

and protection" (Psalm 91:1-4 NLT).

The response required, as noted above, must be imbued with trust and obedience. In the Wesleyan tradition, trust is one of the key ways in which we understand Christian faith. John Wesley was clear that though faith involved belief in certain doctrines (such as the Trinity), it had "a deeper, more demanding dimension— personal trust in God."[28] He realized that you can believe something, but still not trust it.[29]

Yet, faith is about trust. It is about responding to God's gracious love with trust. We trust that God is at work in the world. We trust that through Jesus Christ God does have a plan to save the *whole world*, including us.

The dynamics of trust and obedience define the relational and personal dimensions of faith. Echoing Jesus, Fox and Morris have often rightly pointed out that "we tend to treasure what we trust and trust what we treasure."[30] Christian faith is about placing our ultimate trust in God. Trust is at the core of our response to God.

Obedience follows on the heels of trust and is the ethical out-working of our response to God's grace. If we truly trust God, the treasures of our heart are realigned based on that ultimate trust. Obedience is not only a direct consequence but is also the evidence of true faith.

Several years ago, I traveled to Nigeria to speak to a large gathering of women in a remote area in the northeast part of that country. It was a life-changing experience; yet because I had to travel alone, it was also very frightening. My hosts were gracious and attended to me carefully, lovingly, and with great concern for my safety, but the danger of traveling in that part of Nigeria still pressed in on me.

The day before I left, I had a phone conversation with my parents. Each morning throughout their marriage, they have shared in a time of devotion and prayer. That day, the reading included Psalm 91. They wanted to share it with me as I prepared to travel the next morning.

Psalm 91 echoed in my ears during my entire stay in Nigeria. I found rest in God's shadow and shelter under God's wings. At every point of worry or concern, God placed someone in my path, many times a stranger, who provided exactly the information or insight or care that I needed.

I learned a great deal about myself during those days. The biggest lesson related to trust. Before then, unbeknownst to me, my greatest trust was *not* in God the Father, who sent the Son, in the power of the Holy Spirit. That trust was reserved for me: I trusted in my *own* abilities and capacities, my *own* strengths and talents. The configuration of my trusts placed me at the top with everything flowing outward from there. Yet through that testing time, God realigned my configuration of trusts and awakened in me *ultimate* trust in a way I had never experienced before. That has made all the difference.

How has your trust in God affected the way you order your life?

How has trust led to obedience, where response becomes responsibility?

Is there an area where you are reluctant to trust God?

Understanding Christian faith as a centered, personal, relational response involving trust and obedience provides us with a level of clarity that is essential to authentically showing and sharing the love of Jesus. As we open our arms to initiate embrace, we open them with a keen sense of humility, as those who know their brokenness. And yet we also open them with clarity, unwavering in our knowledge of the source of our healing and hope.

Remembering the essential values of humility and clarity, authentic faith-sharing from a stance of embrace takes the form of a witness. A witness is someone who tells the truth about what they have seen, heard, and experienced. Often, we feel we need to have all the answers about faith, but we will never have all the answers. On this side of glory, no human being will ever have all the answers regarding life or faith. We may be able to have some of the answers, and those answers are likely to be helpful, but there will always be mystery.

Rather than focusing on having all the answers, we need the humility to be honest about our own faith experience and the clarity to understand how our story fits into God's story. In this way, our sharing with others becomes authentic because we are not only sharing our faith, but we are also sharing our life.

As we reach out to others on behalf of Jesus Christ, we stand with our arms open, so that others will know we are with them for the long haul. Willing to explore with them. Ask questions with them. Search for answers with them. Grow with them. And in the space created between us, the Holy Spirit is given freedom to move within us and through us, for healing, for transformation, for redemption.

PRAY ABOUT IT

Reflect on the definition of Christian faith and the way you have experienced it as being a centered, personal, relational response of trust and obedience. Which aspects have been the most meaningful? Which have been the most challenging? Come before God with thanksgiving for God's gracious love, which was pursuing you before you were ever aware, and lay before God whatever challenges in faith you are facing.

ACT ON IT

Reflect on the essential values of humility and clarity as they are represented by the open arms of embrace. What might you need to change for others to perceive you as standing with open arms? What action can you take this week to demonstrate that posture to yourself and others? Make a few notes.

GROUP MEETING ~ **SESSION TWO**

SMALL GROUP EXPERIENCES such as this involve patience—spiritual growth and learning do not happen overnight. Recognize that God is working within you one step at a time, so be open to what God may be seeking to teach you.

The spiritual growth we hope to experience around authentically showing and sharing the love of Jesus depends in part on group participation, so share as openly and honestly as you can. Listen to what others are saying. Sometimes the meaning God intends for us to receive lies beneath the surface. We will benefit only through listening attentively. Remember also that you have a contribution to make to the group. Something that appears trivial or unimportant to you may be exactly what another person in the group needs to hear. Being profound is not the goal; rather, simply share your experience.

OPENING PRAYER

INSIGHTS AND CHALLENGES

Review your notes from the week.

What new insight did you gain?

What challenge did you encounter?

Invite each person to share an insight and a challenge encountered in the material.

SHARING TOGETHER

1. Discuss Jesus' twin practice of renaming and remaking. How have you experienced that practice? How have you witnessed it in the lives of others?
2. Reflect on the image of open arms as an illustration of the humility necessary to show and share the love of Jesus. What challenges do we face in cultivating that kind of humility?

3. Spend a few minutes discussing the difference between humility and timidity or faintheartedness. Do you believe the distinction is important for authentic faith-sharing? Why or why not?

4. Consider the relationship between humility and clarity. How do those essential values complement one another?

5. Review the definition of Christian faith as a centered, personal, relational response of trust and obedience. Was there an element of this definition that challenged or surprised you? If so, why?

6. Close your time of sharing by inviting one person to share their experience of faith. It may be the entire story or just a portion. The reflection questions included in this session move through our basic experience of faith. Reflecting on our responses puts us in touch with our personal story in such a way that we are empowered to share it with confidence and grace.

ACT ON IT

Invite persons to share the change they were challenged to make so that others might perceive them as standing with open arms. What actions will they take this week to demonstrate that posture?

PRAY ABOUT IT

Invite the group to share special prayer concerns. After a time of prayer around those issues, close by praying aloud together:

Dear Jesus,

I thank you that I have been remade and renamed through the power of your Holy Spirit. As I move through this day and the coming days, be alive within me, possessing my mind, heart, and will. As I open my arms to others, fill me with such humility that others are able to see you clearly and glimpse the depth of your love and care. Amen.

EMBRACE:

SESSION THREE
WAITING IN THE POWER OF THE SPIRIT

ESSENTIAL VALUE:

PRAYER

Starting from scratch, he made the entire human race and made the earth hospitable,
with plenty of time and space for living so we could seek after God, and not just grope
around in the dark but actually find him. He doesn't play hide-and-seek with us.
He's not remote; he's near. We live and move in him, can't get away from him!
One of your poets said it well: "We're the God-created."
Acts 17:26-28 (MSG)

WE BEGIN THIS session by focusing on the second stage of our metaphor of embrace—waiting. In the context of the metaphor, waiting is an excellent image for the third essential value of authentically showing and sharing the love of Jesus: prayer.

To initiate an embrace, our arms must first open; yet for an embrace to occur, we must wait, reaching for the other, but not yet touching. [31] This is a significant part of embrace. Open arms begin the movement toward another, but it is not a movement that invades or forces a response. It creates space within us and moves beyond our own boundaries, but it does not cross the boundaries of the other. Rather, it waits for a response, a reciprocal opening of the arms.

Waiting can be difficult, especially in the practice of evangelism, but waiting is the exercise of self-control within ourselves out of respect for the other. Others may not want to be embraced. They may prefer to be left alone. Therefore, for the sake of their integrity, we exercise self-control and wait.

> Waiting is an exercise of self-control within ourselves out of respect for the other, who may not want to be embraced.

Although it may appear imbalanced, waiting with open arms is not an act of powerlessness. Waiting holds within it an internal power, but it is not the power of coercion, manipulation, or a forceful destruction of the boundaries of another. Waiting holds within it the power of vulnerability and openness, undergirded by expectant hope. It is a power that recognizes that without reciprocity, there can be no embrace.

From the perspective of authentically sharing our faith, waiting creates space for the working of the Holy Spirit. When we move back from our own boundaries to make space for another, open our arms, and wait in the power of expectant hope, we open ourselves to the working of the Holy Spirit in the space between us and the other person. Waiting provides the opportunity for discernment on our part and on the part of the other person, a heightened awareness of what the Holy Spirit might be doing within us, within them, and between the two of us.

How have you experienced waiting in your relationships with others? How has the need to wait surfaced in your relationships with those outside the church?

Waiting is focused time, a season of mindfulness when we are deliberately attentive to the movement of the Holy Spirit as we seek to reach others on behalf of Jesus Christ. This may strike many of us as obvious. Of course we want to be in tune with the Holy Spirit. Of course we are praying that people will discover the incredible, life-changing love of God in Jesus Christ. But waiting, and the essential value of prayer that accompanies it, goes much deeper than that.

I enjoy the band Coldplay. A while back, they released a beautiful song called *'Til Kingdom Come*. I am sure thoughts of God were far from the forefront as the lyrics were written, but I believe they capture something very important about the human spiritual condition. Chris Martin sings about needing someone to hold him; longing for someone who understands; someone who really *hears* him. This longing is deep and raw and has gone unfulfilled for years and years. His words resonate not only at the personal level, but also at the spiritual level.

All human beings have a *God-shaped hole* in their hearts. That is what makes us long for God even before we have a name for that longing. We have this inner longing because we are created in the image of a relational, Triune God—Father, Son, and Holy Spirit.

God created human beings to be in relationship. That means that all of us, every human being on the planet, has a longing. We are all searching for intimacy and connection with God and with other people—not because we are Christian, but because we are human.

> Authentic faith-sharing always begins with prayer. Before we ever open our arms, we should be on our knees.

> "O God, you are my God; I earnestly search for you. My soul thirsts for you; my whole body longs for you in this parched and weary land where there is no water" (Psalm 63:1 NLT).

"Therefore, go and make disciples of all the nations, baptizing them in the name of the Father and the Son and the Holy Spirit. Teach these new disciples to obey all the commands I have given you. And be sure of this: I am with you always, even to the end of the age"

(Matthew 28:19-20 NLT).

"Go into all the world and preach the Good News to everyone" (Mark 16:15 NLT).

That longing echoes in the background as Chris Martin sings *'Til Kingdom Come*. It is reflected in Paul's words to the Athenians in the Scripture passage that began this session. It is reflected throughout the psalms. It is reflected in Augustine's profound insight about God, "You have made us for yourself, and our heart is restless until it rests in you." We live in a world filled with people who have named and unnamed yearnings for connection, who are restless and searching and waiting to be set free. They will be restless until they find their rest in God.

Part of maturing in faith is recognizing that we are the ones God has determined to use to help people recognize and name that God-shaped hole within them. That is the truth laid out in the great commissions in Matthew, Mark, and Acts. When we acknowledge that aspect of following Jesus, we become channels through which God's Holy Spirit can move for transformation and redemption. That is what showing and sharing the love of Jesus is all about—creating space within ourselves and between us and others so that they might discover the One who understands, who hears, who sets them free: the only One who can fill that God-shaped hole within them.

Reflect on your journey of faith thus far. How has that been a process of longing for God to fill a hole inside your heart?

How have you seen that longing evidenced in other people?

What is your response to the idea that the various great commissions in Scripture point to our responsibility to become channels of the Holy Spirit?

I mentioned earlier that sharing our faith from a stance of embrace begins with prayer. Prayer saturates our waiting. But it is not prayer in general. Authentic faith-sharing begins with *intercessory prayer*, the kind of prayer that takes us out of ourselves, moves us out of the bubble of our own lives. If we are not actively praying for people, we will never be able to effectively share the gospel with them.

This idea runs much deeper than simply praying that someone accepts Christ—even though that is important. To get at that depth, we need to explore both intercessory prayer and faith-sharing in greater detail.

Like the longing that is part of human nature, prayer is also distinctively human. The need to pray is as natural as our need for food or water. It is the instinctive way we seek to ease our restlessness and attempt to fill the hole within our hearts.

In prayer, we are reaching out to something greater than

> If we are not actively praying for people, we will never be able to effectively share the gospel with them.

Prayer is about the movement

of God in our lives and

in the lives of others.

ourselves. As we do this, it does not take long for our minds to turn to the needs of others. This is because we are made in the image of our Triune God. Because our God is relational, so our praying is relational; it is how we are wired.

Although prayer is natural, it remains filled with mystery. At the heart of this mystery is the truth that for Christians, prayer is about the movement of God in our lives and in the lives of others. This may seem strange to some of us. It is tempting to associate prayer with getting an answer, especially the answer we have in our minds before we begin to pray. It is easy to reduce prayer to a process of getting what we want, when we want it. However, when we give in to that temptation, we often become disappointed, even disillusioned, when things do not turn out as we had hoped. But prayer is about God's movement in our lives and in the lives of others, and that understanding grounds everything else we say about it.

How have you encountered the movement of God in your life through your experience of prayer?

How often do thoughts of others enter your heart and mind through prayer?

When we begin to connect prayer as a movement of God in the lives of others with the idea of becoming a channel for the Holy Spirit, the significance of prayer as an essential value of sharing our faith becomes evident. Because the need to be in relationship is a human need, not only a Christian need, prayer and authentic faith-sharing intersect at our most human point of need—the need for relationship, the need for connection with God and others.

Like prayer, showing and sharing the love of Jesus is about relationship. More specifically, it is about relationships of trust. People need to trust that we care. They need to trust that we love them the way we say we love them, and trust that we are not targeting them or judging them or trying to manipulate them.

During my doctoral studies at the University of Durham in England, a young man joined me as I was eating my evening meal in the St. John's College dining hall. As a middle-aged American woman amidst mostly British twenty-something students, I was a curiosity at St. John's during my visits, and I am sure he was wondering what business had brought me there.

Our conversation began with the usual pleasantries; however, when he discovered I was studying the theology of evangelism, he became quite animated. Apparently during that week, there was a very intense, public thrust of Christian witnessing on the campus. It was clear this young man had little regard for that type of evangelism. He felt it to be overbearing and intrusive. Yet as our conversation progressed, he mentioned he had a Christian friend who had shared quite intimately about his faith journey. In contrast to the public witnessing, this young man was dramatically more receptive to the sharing of his friend.

I asked him to describe his thoughts on the difference between the two experiences. Interestingly, he felt they were very distinct. To him, the public witnessing was evangelism but the sharing of his friend was not. Yet he recognized both his friend and those publicly witnessing provided him with the same information. He could not

> Prayer and authentically sharing our faith intersect at our most human point of need—the need for relationship, the need for connection with God and others.

adequately explain this, even to himself. However, at an intuitive level he knew the answer was in some way related to trust. He could receive information from the friend whom he trusted that he could not receive from strangers making public witness on campus.

The best foundation for authentic faith-sharing is a trusting, caring relationship. Relationships of trust and care allow us space to share our faith and space for the Holy Spirit to work for transformation in our lives and in the lives of those we care about. My young friend at Durham could not receive information about Jesus Christ from people doing public witnessing but he was open to talking to his friend. There was no relationship with the strangers on campus, but because he had a trusting relationship with his friend, he was open to discussing all kinds of deep things of faith.

Relationships of trust and care are fostered by prayer. As we pray for others, we come to see them in a new light and our care for them deepens. Faith can only be shared when a depth of care and trust exists. If we do not care enough about the people we hope to reach for Christ to pray for them, then our commitment to sharing the gospel with them is likely not as deeply rooted as we think.

If we do not care enough about the people we hope to reach for Christ to pray for them, then our commitment to sharing the gospel with them is likely not as deeply rooted as we think.

Reflect on your closest relationships with non-Christian or unchurched friends. How have you incorporated those relationships into your prayer life?

Incorporating those outside our community of faith into our prayers is not simply praying that they come to know Jesus Christ. Yes, that is our ultimate hope, and that desire undergirds our praying. Yet we do not pray that others would accept Christ and then sit back and wait for that to happen. There is much more to intercessory prayer as an essential value of faith-sharing than that. Recognizing this points to the importance of immersing ourselves in the dynamics of intercessory prayer.

Authentically showing and sharing the love of Jesus from a stance of embrace is not about convincing another person. That change of heart comes only through the power of the Holy Spirit. In like manner, we do not pray to convince God. God does not need to be convinced that someone we know needs to become a Christian. God already knows that. In fact, God is likely already at work in that person's life before we ever get involved.

Thus, our praying is not to convince God of the "right or best answer"—whether that be in the life of another or in our own lives. Because we are human, we do not have the wisdom to know what the *truly right* or *best* answer is. We can have inklings. We can have intellectual insight, but that is as close as we can come. More often, however, though we may not know what is right or best, we are quite clear about what we *want*. Unfortunately, what we want, at the moment we want it, is not always the wisest answer.

Early in my marriage, as I was completing my Masters of Divinity at Yale, I believed that God was calling me to pursue a PhD in Theological Ethics. Because my husband was in the middle of his surgical residency, I was limited in my choice of schools, so I applied only to Yale. I fully believed I was following God's leading by pursuing doctoral studies and prayed fervently that God would grant my desire to begin this work. When the acceptance letters were mailed, however, I did not receive one. My application was denied.

Does this story resonate with you? Why or why not? Think about ways your experience of prayer may intersect with mine. Make some notes of your reflections.

Prayer as an essential value of evangelism is not about persuasion. It is about joining in God's movement in our own lives and in the lives of others. When we pray for others, we become connected to what God is doing in their lives. That connection propels our minds and hearts toward God. We become willing to create space for God's Spirit to flow through our prayers to others, speaking to them directly. This is key when we think about authentic faith-sharing.

It is not a matter of cut-and-dried petitions—God please make my friend a Christian. God please let me be accepted to graduate school. It is about being open to the way the Holy Spirit may be working through our prayers, *not only to move others but also to move us.* When we pray for others, we open ourselves to the working of the Holy Spirit in *our own* lives, not just in the lives of those for whom we pray.

That being said, prayer *is* asking. It is a request. But here is the difficult truth: All prayer is answered but not all requests are granted. The mystery here is that there may be a discrepancy between the answer we receive and the answer we want. That was my painful discovery when praying about graduate school.

Karl Barth has said that God cleanses our prayers. God's wisdom permeates the answer we receive. The wisest answer for me and graduate school was not to go at that time, even though I badly wanted to and passionately asked God to make it so. The wisest answer was no, so my request was denied. I did not get what I wanted.

God's no was a crisis for me as I tried to discern my path in ministry. About a month later, however, I realized the wisdom in that answer when I discovered I was pregnant with our third child. The prospects of beginning a PhD program, pregnant, with two children under five, while married to a surgical resident were overwhelming. No was indeed the wisest answer.

This is a crucial point for sharing our faith from a stance of embrace. We are not in control of the times or the seasons. God has granted each of us free will, so all our efforts to reach out to others with the love of Jesus Christ must respect that freedom. As we discussed in our last session, God never forces or coerces and neither do we. We may not see our supplication for another person

> When we pray for others, we open ourselves to the working of the Holy Spirit in *our own* lives, not just in the lives of those for whom we pray.

granted. We may not see the dramatic change we are pleading for. Yet, as I mentioned earlier, when we pray for others, we come to see them in a new light. That is a transformation that takes place within *us*. It is a change in *our* perspective and attitudes, and that is often the most significant first step in God's answer to our prayers. God answers by changing us, which is an answer we do not always recognize.

> When we pray for others, God often answers by first changing us, which is an answer we do not always recognize.

When have you received answers to your prayers that were not what you desired or expected? Make a few notes about that experience.

When you have prayed for others, how have you experienced a change in your perspective or attitude?

It can be painful to experience God's refusal of our requests. It can be painful to experience God's seeming silence in response to our prayers. But just as we must distinguish between denied requests and unanswered prayer, we must make another distinction as well, what some have called the distinction between *faith in prayer* and *prayer in faith*. [32]

Placing our faith in prayer affects our attitude. We are inclined toward ultimatums and a "this is the answer" approach. I prayed to get into graduate school *at that time, in that program, at that school.* When it did not happen, I felt my prayers had failed and as I said, it was a crisis for me on a variety of levels.

Prayer in faith, on the other hand, asks and keeps asking. It may be loud and active. It may be emotional and pleading. But it always involves submission to the will of God. Our faith is not in *prayer;* it is in *God.* [33] What I discovered in my ungranted petition about graduate school was that God's answer was bigger and wiser than I understood when I was pleading.

We may plead passionately for our needs. I believe God *desires* that we implore honestly and passionately. And yet, our faith is in God, so we always close with, "thy will be done." In the context of faith, our confidence comes in the reality that all forces are ultimately under God's reign and power and that God, who is perfect in love, genuinely has our best interest at heart. All things really will work together for good for those who love God. [34] This is especially true for the intercessory prayer that is an essential value for authentic faith-sharing.

As we plead with God on behalf of others, though the answer we receive may be different from what we expect or desire, God *does* respond. God speaks through our minds and gives us new ideas and perspectives, new insights about the person we are praying for—about their hopes and dreams, their struggles and joys. God speaks through our will and gives us new desires or rekindles old passions that have lost vitality, and that gives us power as we reach out to others. God speaks through our emotions, comforting us, calming us, challenging us, making us restless, healing us, giving us peace, stirring us up, troubling us. God speaks through our imagination, through our memory, reminding us of something in the past because it is relevant to our present and future. [35]

> Our faith is not
>
> in *prayer;*
>
> it is in *God.*

Everyone who asks receives a response. It may not always be the response we want, but we don't give up. We reformulate, we refocus, we open ourselves to being searched and purified in our praying. We open ourselves to seeing others in a new light. We wait.

What is your experience of praying for another person, particularly someone who is currently outside the boundary of the church?

How have you come to see others in a new light through your practice of intercessory prayer?

How do waiting and prayer relate to each other? Would you say you are patient in prayer?

When we think about how God works in the world, it is not uncommon to believe that God works through our actions. It is that belief that undergirds much of our ministry on behalf of Jesus Christ. Yet, we struggle with this same concept regarding our prayers. We believe God works through our actions, but we have difficulty believing that God may also work through our prayers. And yet, that is exactly what Scripture tells us.

"Suppose you went to a friend's house at midnight, wanting to borrow three loaves of bread. You say to him, 'A friend of mine has just arrived for a visit, and I have nothing for him to eat.' And suppose he calls out from his bedroom, 'Don't bother me. The door is locked for the night, and my family and I are all in bed. I can't help you.' But I tell you this—though he won't do it for friendship's sake, if you keep knocking long enough, he will get up and give you whatever you need because of your shameless persistence" (Luke 11:5-8 NLT).

Prayer matters. It is the dynamic part of our communion with God. It is the way we become part of God's movement in the world and in people's lives. It is the way we become active participants in the fulfillment of God's kingdom.

A major part of the fulfillment of the kingdom is people coming into restored relationship with God. That is what evangelism is all about. That is why evangelistic intercession is so important. Evangelistic intercession is the type of prayer that grounds our faith-sharing. We are not praying to force people into relationship with God or praying that their freedom be violated. We are praying that they be open to God and the way God desires to move in their lives.

Evangelistic intercession is rooted in willing love. We need to love others enough to pray earnestly for them. When we do that, God often presents opportunities and alternatives that they—or we—may not have otherwise been aware of.

When we intercede evangelistically, *we are calling on God to act in the life of another person.* There are several facets to this calling. First, because Christian prayer is conscious communication with God, we are sharing our deepest needs: not telling God what to do, as we have seen, but sharing needs. Mystery pervades this process as we struggle to share our needs and then leave it to God's wisdom to decide what to do about those needs.

Leaving it to God does not mean we are passive. Believing God knows best and is ordering all things for the best does not mean we stop working for the best God has for us. It is the same with prayer. Our waiting is not passive, but active. We may believe God knows best and is ordering what is best for our loved one, but that does not mean we stop working and praying for our loved one. [36]

Second, we pray that we will be sensitive to the urgent needs of those around us. When we combine the urgent needs of others with the willing love that grounds evangelistic intercession, we begin to grasp the dynamic of this essential value. Jesus' story about

60

the man who went to his friend's house at midnight to ask for bread illustrates this dynamic. The man asks for bread, not for himself, but for the guests who have arrived unexpectedly at his house. Their need, coupled with his willing love to meet that need, send him banging at his neighbor's door in the middle of the night. [37]

As we pray that we will be sensitive to the needs of those around us, we are praying not just about the person's need to be in relationship with God. We must love enough to desire what is best in the *whole* of a person's life, not just in this one area. That is what brings integrity to our praying and to our faith-sharing—love that shows itself in the care for body, mind, and spirit.

A third facet of evangelistic intercession is our helplessness. The man in Jesus' story was willing to give his guests bread, but he did not have any. It was his inability to provide what his guests needed that sent him begging to his friend.

During the last session, we talked about how personal faith is. We can never have faith for another person. We can pray that another would have faith, but we can never have faith for another person. Yet an awareness of our helplessness in this regard is the very strength of our intercession.

Our helplessness leads to supplication. Supplication is when our feeling of need—for ourselves or another—overcomes our grasp of words, when our wrestling becomes so deep that we are led to allow the Holy Spirit to pray for us. Supplication occurs when we come to a place of "utter faith in God to do what we cannot do." [38] Paul describes it in Romans when he says, "The Holy Spirit helps us in our weakness. For example, we don't know what God wants us to pray for. But the Holy Spirit prays for us with groanings that cannot be expressed in words. And the Father who knows all hearts knows what the Spirit is saying, for the Spirit pleads for us believers in harmony with God's own will" (Romans 8:26-27 NLT).

Persistence is the third feature of evangelistic intercession. In Jesus' story the man gets the bread because of his persistence. He

> Supplication occurs when we come to a place of "utter faith in God to do what we cannot do."

keeps on asking. We press, urge, and beg with troublesome persistence. We pray again and again and again. We persist, but not because we do not trust God. Nor do we keep asking because God needs us to ask repeatedly. We persist because there is a cumulative effect of repetition in prayer. Praying again and again allows us to see new facets of need or new facets of our own experience that we might otherwise miss if we had not persevered in our praying. [39]

The final two attributes of our calling on God are unselfishness and confidence. We are not praying for what we want but for what God knows is best for the other person. Our unselfishness is measured by our willingness to extend ourselves in love, at whatever cost, that our prayers may be answered. It is also measured by how we guard ourselves from unconsciously designing an answer for our prayers. We may pray that another would claim faith in Jesus Christ, but we cannot know exactly what that will look like in the life of the other person. Unselfishness calls for a willingness to let go of our predetermined expectations of an answer and a willingness to accept the answer that comes, acknowledging that we are not in control.

This leads to the last attribute, confidence. Although we are not in control of how God is shaping the life of another, we can be confident that God is indeed at work because we trust God's nature. We can be confident that God will respond, and that confidence is rooted in our faith in God's power, God's love, and God's willingness to do what we can't do.

Think about the various facets of evangelistic intercession—our calling upon God to act in the life of another person. In what way do you struggle when you attempt to intercede for others?

Who are the people beyond the boundaries of the church that you need to begin praying for? What might their most urgent needs be in this moment? Make some notes.

If you are unable to bring to mind specific people, reflect on why that might be and what you might do to expand your circle of relationships on behalf of Jesus Christ. Make some notes on your reflections.

PRAY ABOUT IT

Review your list of people and needs. Bring these people and needs before God with confidence that God is already at work and with anticipation for what the Holy Spirit will begin to do in your own life and in the lives of those for whom you are praying.

If you were unable to note specific people, bring your reflections before God and open yourself to the changes God may be leading you to make.

ACT ON IT

Choose one person from your list above. In addition to prayer, identify one concrete way you might reach out to that person.

GROUP MEETING ~ **SESSION THREE**

YOU HAVE NOW had several weeks of sharing, which have hopefully led to a significant amount of "knowing" within your group. Ideally, persons are feeling safe in the group and are more willing to share. Every person brings something special to the group. Others can more fully experience that uniqueness through sharing. Listening is also crucial. It is, as much as any other action, a means of affirmation. As you continue in your time together, be attentive to the rhythm of sharing and listening, encouraging persons to share as they are comfortable and ensuring that all feel heard.

OPENING PRAYER
INSIGHTS AND CHALLENGES

Review the notes you made of your reflections during the week.

What new insight did you gain?

What challenge did you encounter?

Invite each person to share an insight and a challenge encountered in the material.

SHARING TOGETHER

1. Spend a few minutes discussing the group's response to the image of waiting.
2. Review the three great commissions found in Matthew 28, Mark 16, and Acts 1. Discuss the idea that these point to our responsibility to become channels for the movement of the Holy Spirit.
3. Share reflections on the experience of coming to see others in a new light through prayer.
4. Review the facets of evangelistic intercession. Which of these were the most challenging? What additional aspects of evangelistic intercession might be added to this list?

5. Close your time of sharing by inviting someone (other than the person who spoke in Session Two) to tell their experience of faith. It may be the entire story or just a portion.

ACT ON IT

Invite each person to share the concrete way they plan to reach out to another person.

PRAY ABOUT IT

Invite each member of the group to write his or her name and the name of the person they listed as needing evangelistic intercession on an index card. Include any need this person may have. Mix the cards and distribute them to the group to pray over during the coming weeks. Focus prayers not only on the person in need but also on the way God may be using the group member as a means of grace, love, and care.

Spend some time in silent reflection over the cards, with someone praying aloud to conclude your time together.

EMBRACE:

CLOSING OUR ARMS

ESSENTIAL VALUE:

INTEGRITY

For I will not venture to speak of anything except what Christ has accomplished through me to win obedience from the Gentiles, by word and deed, by the power of signs and wonders, by the power of the Spirit of God, so that from Jerusalem and as far around as Illyricum I have fully proclaimed the good news of Christ.
Romans 15:18-19 (NRSV)

INTEGRITY IS COMMONLY defined as "adherence to a code, especially moral or artistic values."[40] This is certainly a bedrock meaning of integrity and is crucial for showing and sharing the love of Jesus. And yet another meaning, the "quality or state of being complete or undivided," or "the state of being whole, entire, or undiminished" is also significant in understanding integrity as the fourth essential value of authentic faith-sharing. I call this kind of integrity *holistic integrity* because it extends beyond simply following a moral code and incorporates the essential values of humility and clarity. It is a cross-shaped aligning of ourselves with Jesus Christ.

The third step in the metaphor of embrace, closing our arms, helps us grasp the importance of holistic integrity to our way of being in the world as followers of Jesus. Closing our arms is the essence of embrace. [41] There is a sense of completeness that comes when the arms close in an embrace. The other person, whom we experienced as absent when we opened our arms in the first stage, is now present. The void is in some way filled.

Integrity: the quality or state of being complete or undivided; the state of being whole, entire, or undiminished

Closing our arms is impossible, however, without the wholeness of integrity, which is built on both humility and clarity. When we are honest with ourselves and others, when they trust that we believe we are no better or worse than they are, the space between us becomes secure enough to lead to the fullness of embrace.

Earlier in my ministry, I was responsible for a Sunday worship service that met in a local theater. Because it was unconventional, it was attractive to many people who had for a variety of reasons felt unwelcome in or alienated by the church. Many were Christian in name only. Others were not Christian but were interested in exploring faith. Several years after leaving that position, I encountered a woman who had attended regularly. As we spoke, she recalled that she was in a confused and unhealthy place in her life during those years. She sensed that I knew this about her and in some ways disagreed with or even disapproved of some of the ways in which she was coping. Much to my relief, she said that this was a good thing, because even though we might not have agreed, she felt there was a place for her no matter what. The *security* of that space had challenged her to seriously reevaluate her life.

Holistic integrity involves the honesty that comes with both humility and clarity. It also involves reciprocity. Closing our arms in embrace once again helps us envision this. Embrace is impossible without reciprocity. We cannot do it alone. Miroslav Volf perceptively points out that "it takes *two* pairs of arms for *one* embrace."[42] A full embrace is both active and passive. We hold and we are held. There may be varying degrees of giving; however, each must enter the space of the other and feel the presence of the other. A full embrace depends on such reciprocity and interchange.

> Embrace must always be reciprocal. It takes two pairs of arms for one embrace.

During my ministry in the local theater, I was surrounded by many people who had felt rejected or unwelcome in other churches. Many were struggling in faith and in life. Many were involved in practices and circumstances that undermined their wholeness. I ministered among these people for eight years, and many of them had a profound effect on me. As I sought to extend open arms to them and create a secure space for the Holy Spirit to move, I felt their response, and it was often a surprising experience of "being held" by them as much as my "holding them." In my conversation with the woman who had attended during those years, she described this mutuality. She said that though she sensed I disagreed, it was important to her that I took her seriously and was *always open to the possibility that she might have something to offer me.* Embrace must always be reciprocal.

Reflect on a relationship in which you do (did) not feel reciprocity. How does (did) the uneven nature of that relationship make you feel?

Reflect on a relationship in your life that is (was) marked by reciprocity, in which you feel (felt) that you are (were) both holding and being held. Make some notes about your feelings and experience.

How do these experiences contrast?

The holistic integrity embodied in embrace also requires a soft touch. We do not grip too tightly, but we also do not melt into each other. In either of those situations, embrace does not exist. If we grip too tightly, the other is overpowered. If we do not grip tightly enough, we can lose ourselves in unhealthy self-denial. Yet, in a full embrace, the identity of each person is both preserved and transformed. The integrity of each is intact, and yet each sees both themselves and the other in a new light.

Evangelism evokes a negative response in no small part, I believe, because we lack a "soft touch." We have all heard stories of the corner evangelist, shouting hellfire and damnation at passersby. Many of us have experienced preachers who conclude their sermons with "altar calls" accompanied by hymns such as *Just As I Am*. The invitation to come forward is, in fact, a soft touch, especially if it includes praying with or in some way making contact with those who have come forward. Unfortunately, that is not always the scenario. Rather, the altar call is accompanied by the preacher gazing intently at all who have not yet responded, announcing that we will sing the last verse *yet again*, to make sure *everyone* has had time to respond. In these situations, the discomfort is often unmistakable.

The tendency to recoil at stories like that is not, however, an excuse for no touch at all. A full embrace requires contact. Invitations are very important. I know of people who say it took them much longer to enter the Christian faith because they were never actually invited to do so. A gentler touch in the context of worship might be for preachers to provide a variety of opportunities for people to respond, whether by coming forward to the altar or speaking privately after the service, and then to model a response through their own presence at the altar in prayer.

Like waiting, a gentle touch also allows others space to freely respond. Holistic integrity as a core value of authentic evangelism is not only about our integrity. It is about the integrity of others as well. Like waiting, a gentle touch respects our own integrity as well as the integrity of others. It allows others to feel secure, and it allows room for the transforming power of the Holy Spirit.

Most Christians believe in the Holy Spirit's power to transform. However, when we share our faith, often we assume that the other person is the one being transformed rather than us. We share the gospel with expectant hope that *others* might be transformed, at the bare minimum, into persons who profess faith in Jesus Christ as Lord and Savior. At times, our assumptions can go a bit further and involve others being transformed into Christians who resemble us, thinking and believing exactly like we do. Thus, recognizing the transformative power of embrace for *both selves* is crucial to our understanding of holistic integrity. Showing and sharing the love of Jesus must always involve openness to the power of the Holy Spirit to continually work not only through us toward others but also through others toward us. In this way, God works for integrity and wholeness for all.

Describe your expectations when you think of faith-sharing.

Do your expectations include your own inner transformation? Why or why not?

How do we balance invitation and sensitivity?

How might your approach to or understanding of faith-sharing change if you were open to the Holy Spirit's movement in both directions?

As we move toward a deeper understanding of the essential value of holistic integrity, it is helpful to recall that the task of evangelism is the ongoing process of making the good news of the kingdom of God—the gospel—known to others. That means that evangelism is never present unless the good news of the kingdom of God is present. [43]

A common mistake that undermines our integrity, and the integrity of others, is to equate evangelism with conversion. They are not the same. Authentic evangelism is *not* conversion. *The Faith-Sharing New Testament* gives us an excellent definition of conversion: Christian conversion is "the change that God works in us as we respond to God's grace in repentance and faith." [44]

God is responsible for conversion. When it comes to evangelism, we are only responsible for making the gospel known. This is a liberating concept—for both pastors and laypeople. We are not responsible for making converts. We may desire conversion to happen. We may pray fervently as we discussed during our last session, but it is not within our power to make it happen.

Letting go of the responsibility to convert enhances our ability to grasp the reciprocity and gentle touch necessary for our own integrity and the integrity of others. It is better to stop worrying about the *results* of our faith-sharing and instead worry about whether we have *truly made the gospel known* in our relationships with others. The results are in God's hands. Releasing the responsibility for conversion also enables us to see that evangelism is never something we do *to people*. It is something we do *with* the gospel. We make the gospel known. [45]

How would your understanding of evangelism change if you began to think of it as something we do *with the gospel* (make it known) rather than *to people* (convert)?

It is better to stop worrying about the *results* of our evangelizing and instead worry about whether we have *truly made the gospel known* in our relationships with others. The results are in God's hands.

The holistic integrity reflected in the image of arms closing in a full embrace relates to respect for others through reciprocity and a gentle touch. It relates to our own integrity as well. A sense of wholeness must infuse whatever evangelistic practices we undertake.

If we think of showing and sharing the love of Jesus as making the gospel known, the way in which we make it known is important. Sharing our faith will be grounded in holistic integrity; therefore, we make the gospel known in a way that reflects the completeness of our lives. A way to understand this is that we make the gospel known through word, deed, and sign. Empowered by the Holy Spirit, we share the good news of Jesus Christ through our words, through our deeds, and through the signs that the Holy Spirit makes evident in our midst. And as the metaphor of embrace illustrates, we wait and watch in respectful humility and work with expectant hope. [46]

There are several significant aspects to this holistic concept of making the gospel known. We will explore the idea of sign in our next session. At this point, however, we will look more closely at word and deed. The rhythm of this is important. We must offer the gospel in ways that are both verbal *and* visible. Our words must always ring true to our lifestyle, and our life must always support our words. We verbalize the gospel as we are doing it. In this way, authentic faith-sharing occurs in the context of ministries of healing, teaching, serving, nurturing, liberating, reforming, and empowering. [47]

Because the announcement of the kingdom is both verbal and visible, my mentor, Eddie Fox, would often say that asking which is more important is like asking which is more essential, breathing in or breathing out. His answer? It depends on which you did last! We are called to offer a cup of cold water in Jesus' name. Many times, we only offer the name and are dismissed as irrelevant and disconnected. Yet if we only offer the water, we will quench a physical thirst but leave the spiritual thirst unsatisfied. [48]

In many parts of the world, especially in the United States, it is far easier to only offer a cup of cold water. Christians and non-Christians alike do that. We become much more vulnerable as Christians, however, when we begin to speak the deepest convictions of our lives, placing them in front of others and risking their response.

"For I will not venture to speak of anything except what Christ has accomplished through me to win obedience from the Gentiles, by word and deed, by the power of signs and wonders, by the power of the Spirit of God, so that from Jerusalem and as far around as Illyricum I have fully proclaimed the good news of Christ"

(Romans 15:18-19 NRSV).

Which do you find more comfortable, making the gospel known through your words or through your deeds? Why?

How would you and your church approach evangelism differently if you gained a better balance between word and deed?

As we make the gospel known through the rhythm of word and deed, several principles keep us closely tied to the essential value of holistic integrity. We hinted at the first principle in our discussion of prayer. Like intercessory prayer, showing and sharing the love of Jesus does not focus on convincing another person of something. It does not depend on airtight arguments regarding doctrinal propositions. Sharing our faith from a stance of embrace points others to the center of Christian faith, Jesus Christ. It creates space for the Holy Spirit of Jesus to move for transformation, within others, within us, and between us and others.

When we verbally point others to Jesus, it is always in the first person. That is the second principle of authentic faith-sharing grounded in holistic integrity. When we share our faith with

Authentic evangelism points people to the center of Christian faith: Jesus Christ.

Authentic faith-sharing is always in the first person.

another, we always share in the first person.[49] Making the gospel known through the rhythm of word and deed does not require mastery of complex theological concepts; it is simply sharing God's story in light of our own stories—sharing what has happened and is happening in our life of faith.

For some of us, theological reflection and intellectual inquiry is at the heart of our story of faith. For others, it begins with our experience and gains clarity as we engage Christian faith more deeply. Because each of us is unique, God deals uniquely with each of us in ways that empower us to see, hear, and respond. That is why when we speak, we begin by speaking in the first person: *This is what Christ has done in my life.* Sometimes that means sharing our whole story and sometimes it means sharing a part. Sometimes that means beginning with our own story and moving to deeper issues of faith. Regardless of how it unfolds, the importance of sharing in the first person cannot be overstated because we are not telling others what *they should believe,* we are telling them *what we believe* and most importantly, *who we trust.* We are daring to share our experience of God's grace in our own life. [50]

> We are not telling others *what they should believe,* we are telling them *what we believe* and most importantly, *who we trust.*

Have you had the opportunity to share your faith story with another person? If yes, make some notes on the experience. If no, reflect on how you might feel were the opportunity to arise.

The definition of Christian faith discussed in Session Two (a centered, personal, relational response of trust and obedience) provides a way of framing how our stories intersect God's story. How might using that framework bring clarity to your experience of God's grace and enable you to share it with greater confidence?

As we share our faith, the rhythm of word and deed can be seen when we heed the third principle, listening. The act of listening embodies the reciprocity of holistic integrity. It is evidence that we believe others have something to offer us, that what they have to say is valuable—that *they* are valuable.

Compassionate listening creates the space necessary for the movement of the Holy Spirit. It is a whole-body activity that involves not only our ears but also our eyes and hearts.[51] It grounds us not only in the essential value of holistic integrity but also in the essential value of prayer. We listen when we pray, and we listen in our relationships with others. As the saying goes, God created us with two ears and one mouth, which should tell us something about the importance of listening to showing and sharing the love of Jesus.

The fourth principle that binds us to the essential value of holistic integrity is love. In a sense, this has grounded everything we have said thus far. Love undergirds our humility. It is the lens through which we gain clarity; willing love is integral to intercessory prayer. It is our love for others that causes us to open our arms in the first place and supports us as we exercise the self-control of waiting. Love is the reason we can embrace at all.

One final principle highlights the integrated rhythm of word and deed that marks faith-sharing grounded in embrace. At WME,

"Love is patient; love is kind; love is not envious or boastful or arrogant or rude. . . . It bears all things, believes all things, hopes all things, endures all things" (1 Corinthians 13:4-5, 7 NRSV).

Compassionate listening creates space for the movement of the Holy Spirit—within us, within others, and between us and others.

we call it *entering in*. Showing and sharing the love of Jesus is a process of entering the lives of others.[52] Our open arms create space for others. When the Holy Spirit begins to move, the space is perceived as secure; others are drawn to it and feel safe to open their arms. When our arms meet in embrace, the Holy Spirit continues its good work and we are able to learn, love, and care. As we invite others into our lives and enter the lives of others, there is a reciprocal sharing of genuine hopes and dreams, struggle and fear, joy and sorrow.

There are sufficient resources in the gospel to meet every aspect of being human.

Our model is Jesus, who was always focused on people. He saw someone who was sick. He found Zacchaeus in a tree. He reached out to the woman at the well. He noticed children. His entire life was about seeing, hearing, and understanding people—entering in. Rooted in prayer and with clarity, humility, and integrity of purpose, Jesus entered people's worlds and each time he did, he used it as an opportunity to offer good news.

God's grace is good news in all kinds of circumstances, for all kinds of needs. That is the beauty of the gospel. It is multifaceted good news that addresses the multifaceted dynamic of being human. When we enter the lives of others with our identity and purpose clear and whole, we can be confident that there are sufficient resources in the gospel to meet every aspect of being human.[53]

Reflect on the concept of entering in. What do you find most challenging about this idea?

To pull the various aspects of our discussion on integrity together, I believe it is important to return to the witness of Jesus. In becoming human, Jesus temporarily gave up the power connected to his nature as God. Before ever mentioning a word about eternal salvation, Jesus entered into the real agony of human suffering. Showing and sharing the love of Jesus is most deeply rooted in the essential value of holistic integrity, as well as humility, when we maintain a profound awareness of the unredeemed and broken nature of the world. We do not keep this knowledge before us by viewing the church as an isolated island of redeemed souls. We do not keep it before us by focusing on an otherworldly image of redemption involving only human beings in a disembodied afterlife. Redemption does not take place in a purely invisible, interior, privatized sphere. Therefore, Christians can never stop suffering over the unredeemed and broken state of the world.

> Redemption does not take place in a purely invisible, interior, privatized sphere. Therefore, Christians can never stop suffering over the unredeemed and broken state of the world.

As we considered in Session Two, Christian faith is centered on Jesus of Nazareth. He is the one in whom and through whom God's kingdom on earth has begun—a kingdom in which all are given the opportunity to participate. If we worship Christ as God, if we understand the church as the kingdom, if we are aware of God's forgiveness but do not suffer from the continued unredeemed and broken condition of the world, our faith becomes only a shadow of itself. It is at the intersection of our awareness of God's forgiveness and our awareness of the painful reality of the unredeemed and broken condition of the world that faith-sharing gains its authenticity and integrity.

The essential value of holistic integrity and the rhythm of word and deed move us to model Jesus and enter the realities of human existence. We celebrate the joys but also make an honest accounting of the misery, evil, and suffering. We dare not witness to a salvation that applies only to the eternal situation of the human soul, while ignoring the actual, practical, human situations of real misery. Rather, when we show and share the love of Jesus, we must

> We dare not witness to a salvation that applies only to the eternal situation of the human soul, while ignoring the actual, practical, human situations of real misery.

remain immersed in the real lives of people and reflect a deep commitment to their experience of abundant life, not simply in eternity, but in the here and now.

In many societies, but particularly in the United States where religion is now viewed as private, there is great temptation to understand the salvation begun in Jesus Christ as the private salvation of the individual soul with no connection to the realities of the world. Succumbing to that temptation ignores the essential value of holistic integrity and creates a gap between word and deed. Further, this leaves the economic, social, and political sins of human beings not only without liberating criticism but also without the saving hope of the gospel. Yet authentic faith-sharing, when grounded in the essential value of holistic integrity and firmly planted in a stance of embrace, witnesses to the truth of our Triune God revealed in Jesus: "Salvation is whole salvation and the salvation of the whole, or it is not God's salvation." [54]

PRAY ABOUT IT

Review the list of people you created in Session Three. Lift these names up in prayer and ask God to guide you in how you might enter their world in a genuine way.

ACT ON IT

In the King James Version of Philippians, Paul advises us to "let your conversation be as it becometh the gospel of Christ" (Philippians 1:27). Newer versions translate this verse, "Live as citizens of heaven, conducting yourselves in a manner worthy of the Good News about Christ" (NLT). In the Elizabethan English of the King James Version, life and conversation are two ways of speaking about the same thing. As you go about the coming days, keep this verse in the forefront of your mind as an example of the integrated rhythm of word and deed necessary to authentically show and share the love of Jesus.

GROUP MEETING ~ **SESSION FOUR**

LIFE IS FOUND in communion with God and in conversation with others. Listening and responding to what we hear is very important. To really hear others helps them to think clearly and gain perspective. It is life producing. When we speak in ways that make a difference, we speak for the sake of others and thus contribute to the process of wholeness.

OPENING PRAYER

INSIGHTS AND CHALLENGES

Review the notes you made of your reflections during the week.

What new insight did you gain?

What challenge did you encounter?

Invite each person to share an insight and a challenge encountered in the material.

SHARING TOGETHER

1. Discuss the concept of reciprocity and the idea that in the process of authentic faith-sharing the Holy Spirit moves in two directions.
2. Spend some time reflecting on the difference between evangelism and conversion. How does our approach change when we begin to think of evangelism as something we do *with the gospel* rather than something we do *to people*?
3. Consider the group's responses to the idea that sharing our faith includes the rhythm of word and deed. What changes might such a concept lead to in our lives and churches?
4. Review the principles associated with the rhythm of word and deed. Which of these had you not thought of before? Which seemed most challenging?

5. Close your time of sharing by inviting someone (other than the persons who spoke in Sessions Two and Three) to tell their experience of faith. It may be the entire story or just a portion.

ACT ON IT

Following the pattern of Session Three, invite each member of the group to write his or her name and the name of the person they listed as needing evangelistic intercession on an index card. Include the way in which group members hope to enter more genuinely into the life of the person for whom they are praying. Mix the cards and distribute them to the group to pray over during the coming weeks.

PRAY ABOUT IT

Spend some time in silent reflection over the cards that have been distributed. Close your time together by once again praying aloud the Prayer of St. Francis:

Lord, make me an instrument of your peace;
   where there is hatred, let me sow love;
   where there is injury, pardon;
   where there is doubt, faith;
   where there is despair, hope;
   where there is darkness, light;
   and where there is sadness, joy.
O Divine Master, grant that I may not so much seek
   to be consoled as to console;
   to be understood as to understand;
   to be loved as to love;
   for it is in giving that we receive;
   it is in pardoning that we are pardoned;
   and it is in dying that we are born to eternal life. Amen.

EMBRACE:

OPENING OUR ARMS AGAIN

ESSENTIAL VALUE:

WORSHIP

*But the time is coming—indeed it's here now—when true worshipers will worship the
Father in spirit and in truth. The Father is looking for those who will worship him that way.
For God is Spirit, so those who worship him must worship in spirit and in truth.*
John 4:23-24 (NLT)

DURING OUR LAST session, we discussed the rhythm of word and deed that marks holistic integrity as
an essential value of showing and sharing the love of Jesus. There is a third aspect—sign—that we mentioned briefly but now turn to with greater attention. We make the gospel known holistically, through
word, deed, and sign. The role of word and deed is not difficult to accept; yet signs are often trivialized,
misused, or made to look illegitimate. [55] Particularly in the Western nations of the world, many people

are uncomfortable with the idea of signs and wonders reflected in Romans 15:18-19. But as E. F. Harrison has said, signs are simply "visible tokens of invisible realities that are spiritually significant."[56]

Things become signs through the power of the Holy Spirit. Signs include everything from something as amazing as miraculous healings to something as seemingly ordinary as art or music, or as outwardly routine as our ongoing practice of Holy Communion. They are manifestations of the Holy Spirit that enable us to recognize Jesus for who he is. They awaken us to the inbreaking of God's kingdom in our midst. Although they fill our individual lives and spiritual experiences, signs can frequently be seen most fully in the context of the gathered, worshiping community of faith. Therefore, worship is an essential value of authentic faith-sharing.

The final stage of embrace, opening our arms again, hints at the importance that signs and worship signify. Though the Holy Spirit is moving even before we open our arms in the first stage, and then continues to move throughout embrace, it is only at the completion of embrace that we recognize the Spirit's work. For an embrace to be complete, our arms must always open again.[57] Embrace never creates one merged body out of two. Rather, the Holy Spirit preserves the identity of each person even as the imprint of each remains on the other and each experiences the presence of the Spirit.

My grandmother loved gardenia perfume. Some of my fondest memories are of her gentle hugs and the lingering scent of gardenia that would remain on my clothes afterward. Embrace respects our individual identities, but the warm scent remains. It always leaves an imprint as the Holy Spirit moves for transformation.

There is also a circular movement to embrace. The open arms that let the other go in the final stage are the same open arms that in the first stage signal a desire for the other's presence, create space, open boundaries, and issue an invitation. They are the same arms that wait, and then encircle the other's body. The end of an

> "Signs are visible tokens of invisible realities that are spiritually significant."

> Signs are those manifestations of the Holy Spirit that enable us to recognize Jesus for who he is. They awaken us to the inbreaking of God's kingdom in our midst.

embrace is, in a sense, already the beginning of a new embrace, even if the new one might not take place right away.

The circular nature of embrace mirrors the ongoing nature of the Holy Spirit's work in our lives and world, as well as the ongoing nature of showing and sharing the love of Jesus. It is not a one-time thing but is more often an ongoing process as people are loved, welcomed, and nurtured in faith. This makes the worshiping life of the community significant because it is an important aspect of the communal dimension of Christian faith. It is also a principal context for welcoming and nurturing people in faith. What is more, this circular movement points to the expectation that having experienced embrace, each of us will go on to be a transforming presence in the lives of others. Embrace assumes a transformative process of people becoming disciples, who then make disciples, who then make disciples . . . and so on.

This is noteworthy because frequently the focus in our local churches quickly shifts from evangelism to discipleship. Churches reach out to others and seek to make them more fully a part through discipleship ministries that encourage spiritual maturity. This is, of course, very important. However, what we frequently leave out of our approach to discipleship is the idea that having experienced embrace, we then move out to embrace others. As churches guide those new to the faith, a better balance would be to emphasize that embrace is not static or isolated. It is a dynamic process in which each person is transformed and moves outward as a channel of continued transformation. For our discipleship and evangelism to reflect the wholeness of the gospel, we must recognize an important truth. We receive the fullness of God's grace only when we are willing to be made into vehicles of God's grace to others. What happens *to* us must be done *by* us. Because we have been embraced by God, we must embrace others, make space for them, and invite them in. [58]

> We receive the fullness of God's grace only when we are willing to be made into vehicles of God's grace to others. What happens *to* us must be done *by* us. Because we have been embraced by God, we must embrace others, make space for them, and invite them in.

Reflect on your experience of discipleship in your community of faith. What connections have been made between personal growth within and outward transformation beyond?

The gathered community of faith

provides the environment for some

of the Holy Spirit's most powerful

work as people are healed,

reconciled, and forgiven.

Throughout our time together, we have emphasized that it is the movement and power of the Holy Spirit that stimulates change. We are not the source of transformation. It is not within our control to orchestrate another's conversion. We are completely dependent on God's Holy Spirit to go ahead of us as we develop relationships of trust and share our stories of faith. We are completely dependent on God's Holy Spirit to move within us and between us as we walk with others on their spiritual journeys. When we place our trust in the Holy Spirit to work in and through our relationships, and when we wait and work in expectant hope, God uses us in powerful ways.

We should not, however, assume that personal relationships are the only context for sharing faith. The gathered community of faith is an integral part of this process. The gathered community is the environment for some of the Holy Spirit's most powerful work as people are healed, reconciled, and forgiven. Our personal relationships are a rope that others might grasp as they make their way into the community of faith. And yet, it is frequently in the context of the gathered, worshiping community that the Holy Spirit works in powerful and tangible ways for new birth, nurture, and sanctification.

This is why worship is an essential value of authentically showing and sharing the love of Jesus. The circular nature of faith-sharing grounded in embrace points to the ongoing movement of the Holy Spirit as we welcome and nurture in the context of the gathered community of faith. It is in this environment that the Holy Spirit points most clearly to Jesus and awakens within believers an awareness of the inbreaking of God's kingdom. Yet, our worship practices are as varied as our cultures, so worship as an essential value of authentic evangelism is not about the *specifics* of our services—whether we use guitars or organs, whether we worship for one hour or longer. It is about the *dynamic created* when the presence of the Holy Spirit permeates those gatherings.

Because the presence and power of the Holy Spirit are the key components of worship as an essential value of sharing faith, it is important to understand the work of the Holy Spirit. However, as with so much of Christian faith, there is the danger of confusion in this arena. In current Western culture, the term "spirit" has become somewhat meaningless. Often it is associated more with the psychological arena, paranormal activity, or even marketing strategies. In many Western countries, religious understandings of "spirit" have been so influenced by individualistic New Age movements that "spirituality" often simply indicates a form of self-expression. In this kind of environment, it is easy for the term "Holy Spirit" to become separated from its biblical foundations and lose its deep connection with God the Father and Jesus Christ the Son. Additionally, if our understanding of the Spirit is too widespread or ever-present, it becomes difficult for us to discern the Spirit's absence. But discerning the Spirit's absence is crucial. If we are unable to accept the possibility that there may be places or occasions that God's Holy Spirit does *not* inhabit or endorse, then we lose our ability to engage the world with the gospel. [59]

What is your response to the above description of associations with the word "spirit"? How do these interpretations fit into your experience?

Refresh your memory by rereading the section on the Holy Spirit in our first session. Make a few notes on your insights from that session and any new insights you may have gained.

Considering the description in our first session, what is your response to the idea that there are places or occasions that God's Holy Spirit does not inhabit?

From the Wesleyan perspective,

God's Holy Spirit is a *present reality*.

It is the same Spirit who at Pentecost

empowered the followers of Jesus

to leave their hiding places and

boldly proclaim what they had seen

and experienced.

Contemplating the idea that the Holy Spirit may be absent from certain places or occasions raises a second point of confusion. This confusion has become more visible in our current context of globalization. It is a "mono-spirit" understanding of the spiritual world, and it is very unhelpful. From this perspective, the world contains only one spirit, the Holy Spirit of God. All other spirits are pushed into the sphere of superstition.

This view of the world, where there is only God and human beings, is an especially Western Christian understanding, but it is *not* the worldview of the New Testament. It also does not reflect the overall experience of being human, which involves a daily struggle with powerful, often unseen, and apparently inexplicable forces.

In contrast, a full understanding of God's Spirit involves taking evil seriously. Evil exists and stands in opposition to God. This is a difficult stance to take because it often conflicts with the dominant Western worldview. Christians in North America, Europe, and other westernized parts of the world can learn a great deal from our brothers and sisters in Africa, Latin America, and Asia in this regard. James Dunn has a perceptive word, "The New Testament world of demons and spirits is also the biblical world of the Holy Spirit.... In abandoning the dimension of the demonic we may find that we have abandoned also the dimension of the Spirit." [60]

Recognizing that there are a variety of forces at work in the world is especially significant for showing and sharing the love of Jesus. As the twenty-first century continues to unfold, rationality remains a tool to understand the human experience in the world. However, *it is no longer seen as the only tool, or even the best tool*, to understand the powerful, seemingly incomprehensible forces humans encounter in their lives. Faith, on the other hand, is uniquely suited to meet those challenges. Particularly from the Wesleyan perspective, God's Holy Spirit is a *present reality*. It is the same Spirit who at Pentecost empowered the followers of Jesus to leave their hiding places and boldly proclaim what they had seen and experienced. It is the same Spirit who continues to surprise us by speaking, healing, and manifesting God's presence in remarkable and often mindboggling ways. [61] And yet, if we live as though that Spirit is the only one, as though forces in opposition to God do not exist, we risk losing the ability to recognize God's Holy Spirit as a tangible presence in our everyday life. And our everyday life is the very place where we struggle with those powerful, often unseen, and frequently incomprehensible forces. [62]

Because a "mono-spirit" understanding, where there is only God and human beings, is so widespread in Western Christianity, many of us may be challenged by the idea that other forces exist that are in opposition to God. What is your response to this idea?

If this idea is foreign to you, how might engaging this idea more fully change how you approach life and faith?

How might it change how you discern God's Holy Spirit in your daily life?

How might it change how you respond to others, especially those who are struggling?

"Anyone who belongs to Christ has

become a new person. The old life

is gone; a new life has begun!"

(2 Corinthians 5:17 NLT).

"With eager hope, the creation

looks forward to the day when it

will join God's children in glorious

freedom from death and decay"

(Romans 8:20-21 NLT).

Avoiding these two misunderstandings—an overly generalized concept of "spirit" and discounting the presence of other forces active in our world—helps us see an important truth more clearly. The Holy Spirit's work in our lives and our world anticipates God's transformation of the entire universe in new creation. Further, experiences of the Holy Spirit move us to cooperate with God's mission as we reach out to others through authentic faith-sharing and stand with others in solidarity as we serve the sick, the poor, and the downtrodden.

The worshiping life of the gathered community of faith is, in a wide variety of ways, a significant witness to God's anticipated transformation of all creation. As we gather to proclaim and practice the forgiveness of sins through the power of the Holy Spirit, our worship provides a glimpse of God's future, where relationships and people are healed, reconciled, and made new. When we celebrate the Sabbath together, we embody God's new creation—the decisive time when God will come to rest in God's creation, and all of creation will participate in God's rest. When we celebrate Sunday as the feast of the resurrection, we are proclaiming the dawning of God's new creation where resurrection light fills creation and all of reality. We illustrate that redemption is not merely an individual, privatized experience, but is a creation-wide experience of wholeness and community. As we worship together, the light of God's salvation shines on all of creation as it groans under the weight of evil, and it secures the promise that the entire universe (humanity included) will be restored as the world without end.

In addition to witnessing to the all-creation nature of salvation, our communal, worshiping life together provides for the personal experience of God's presence. God's Holy Spirit goes before everything else, moving within us and beyond us. Therefore, through the presence of the Spirit we are empowered to believe, and love, and serve. And it is through the presence of the Holy Spirit amidst the worshiping community that we can participate, at least in a partial way, in the very life of God.

This is significant for showing and sharing the love of Jesus. Dependence on the life-changing presence of God's Holy Spirit is crucial because worship is engagement, not observation. People will not experience healing if we do not offer it. People will not respond if we do not preach for it. People will not receive forgiveness, reconciliation, mercy, love, or grace if we do not create space and time for these to occur. When the worshiping community is reduced to players and observers, it reflects our failure to take seriously the power available through a wholehearted reliance on the Holy Spirit's leading. And yet, when we allow our worship to be in step with the urging of the Spirit, our communal praise, prayer, and proclamation are empowered to become channels of the concentrated, focused Spirit of the Triune God—and lives are changed.

> When we allow our worship to be in step with the urging of the Spirit, our communal praise, prayer, and proclamation are empowered to become channels of the concentrated, focused Spirit of the Triune God.

What new insight did you gain regarding the presence of the Holy Spirit in the worshiping community?

How might your approach to worship change if you were to see it as a channel for the Holy Spirit's work of transformation?

PRAY ABOUT IT

Bring your experience of worship before God—your perception of it, your engagement with it. Reflect on ways you might deepen your experience of worship and your openness to the Holy Spirit to move in that context.

ACT ON IT

Be alert for ways in which God may be turning ordinary aspects of your day into signs that awaken you to the inbreaking of God's kingdom in new ways.

GROUP MEETING ~ **SESSION FIVE**

YOU ARE DRAWING to the close of your study with only one more planned group meeting. Your group may want to discuss the future. Would the group like to stay together for a longer period? Are there resources (books, DVDs, etc.) that the group might desire to use together? As we think about the circular nature of faith-sharing rooted in embrace, are there members of the group who are interested in going deeper in their exploration of evangelism by becoming equipped to lead others in training? World Methodist Evangelism provides training for those who are interested in further study or in teaching on behalf of WME across the Wesleyan family in all parts of the world. You can visit www .worldmethodist.org/embrace for additional information. Test the group to see if they would like to discuss future possibilities.

OPENING PRAYER
INSIGHTS AND CHALLENGES

Review the notes you made of your reflections during the week.
What new insight did you gain?
What challenge did you encounter?
Invite each person to share an insight and a challenge encountered in the material.

SHARING TOGETHER

1. Discuss the idea that signs are manifestations of the Holy Spirit that enable us to recognize Jesus for who he is. What are some signs that have been meaningful in pointing you to Jesus? What signs did you notice during this past week?
2. Think about the circular nature of embrace. How have evangelism and discipleship fit together in your experience of faith?

3. Consider group members' responses to the assertion that there are places and occasions that God's Holy Spirit does not inhabit.

4. Share responses to the idea that other forces exist that are in opposition to God. How does that change our approach to life and faith? How does that impact our discernment of God's Holy Spirit in our daily lives? How does it affect how we respond to others?

5. Discuss the idea that worship is to be an environment of transformation through the power of God's Holy Spirit. What might need to change in your context for that to become more evident?

6. Close your time together by inviting someone who has not yet had the opportunity to share their experience of faith. It may be the entire story or just a portion.

ACT ON IT

Continue to be alert for ways in which God's Holy Spirit is changing ordinary things into signs to bring significance to Christ.

PRAY ABOUT IT

Spend some time sharing about the experience of praying for the persons named on the index cards that have been distributed during the last two weeks. What new insights have come through your praying? Enter a time of prayer over the issues raised in this sharing and the ongoing needs of the people listed on the cards. Persons may pray aloud as they feel led. Invite someone to conclude with a closing prayer.

EMBRACE:

SESSION SIX

ABUNDANT LIFE

ESSENTIAL VALUE:

URGENCY

I am the gate. Whoever enters by me will be saved, and will come in and go out and find pasture. The thief comes only to steal and kill and destroy. I came that they may have life, and have it abundantly.
John 10:9-10 (NRSV)

Those who drink the water I give will never be thirsty again. It becomes a fresh, bubbling spring within them, giving them eternal life.
John 4:14 (NLT)

Now repent of your sins and turn to God, so that your sins may be wiped away. Then times of refreshment will come from the presence of the Lord, and he will again send you Jesus, your appointed Messiah. For he must remain in heaven until the time for the final restoration of all things, as God promised long ago through his holy prophets.
Acts 3:19-21 (NLT)

WE CLOSE OUR time together by exploring the sixth essential value of showing and sharing the love of Jesus: urgency. When it comes to authentic faith-sharing, we are speaking of a very specific type of urgency—a bold urgency. It might also be thought of as an urgent boldness. When something is urgent, it requires immediate action or attention. When people are bold, they exhibit courage and confidence. There is an urgent need to share the good news, demanding our immediate action and attention. To meet this urgent need, we must have boldness; we must be confident and courageous as we share.

One of the striking marks of Christian faith is that it holds together several important concepts that seem to be in opposition. For instance, the earthly and the eternal, the particular and the universal, the temporal and the eschatological (a big word pointing to the end when God's kingdom will finally come in all its fullness). The urgency and boldness that mark showing and sharing the love of Jesus relate most specifically to the earthly and the eternal.

During our study, we highlighted that salvation in Jesus Christ is whole-creation salvation. Our redemption involves not just the promise of eternal life yet to come but also the promise of abundant life that begins even now. Thus, not only is there an eternal urgency, there is an earthly urgency as well. The good news is good not only because God desires human flourishing in God's eternal future but also because God desires human flourishing *now*.

> The good news is good not only because God desires human flourishing in God's eternal future but also because God desires human flourishing *now*.

Have you thought about faith-sharing in terms of urgency? Why or why not? Make some notes about your thoughts.

When you have thought about the urgent need to share the good news, what has been the nature of the urgency?

In Session Three, we talked about the God-shaped hole within all humans that causes them to long for connection and relationship. Because God created us in God's own image, humans are relational. To flourish, we need to be in relationship with God and with others. This is not a twenty-first-century need. It is a human need that existed during the early days of the church, just as it exists today. When Paul was preaching in Athens, he was troubled by how much they were struggling to find their way. They had idols for everything, gods for every taste and style. There was even an altar to the unknown god (Acts 17:16-34).

The church in John Wesley's day was also surrounded by people spiritually searching. Wesley recognized their yearnings and boldly offered them the gospel in every circumstance he found himself, with every kind of person he encountered: rich, poor, working class, middle class. Our yearning for connection and relationship, then, is not tied to culture, place, or time, but to being human.

Given this natural human longing, it is interesting that our world has about the same percentage of Christians as it did at the beginning of the twentieth century. Approximately one-third of the world's population was Christian in 1910, and approximately one-third is Christian now. There are many differences between our world in 1910 and our world now. However, when it comes to evangelism and faith-sharing, one of biggest differences is attitude. In 1910, Christians from around the world gathered in Edinburgh, Scotland, for the World Missionary Conference. While there, they *lamented* that only one-third of the world was Christian. That fact was the cause of deep pain and led to the urgent call to "win the world for Christ in this generation!" That is a striking contrast to the 2010 gathering that marked the 100-year anniversary of the conference. At the 2010 gathering, they *celebrated* that one-third of the world was Christian.

Reflect on the contrast between lamenting that *only* one-third of the world is Christian and celebrating that one-third of the world is Christian. Make some notes on your thoughts.

From lament to celebration. That is a substantial shift in attitude regarding the same information. That shift should be a significant red flag for all Christians, but especially those of us in the Wesleyan traditions who have Great Awakenings in our DNA. It points to the need for us to reclaim a sense of urgency and a burning desire to spread the good news of Jesus Christ across the planet.

A few years ago, secular scholar and writer Charles Murray gave a lecture on public policy titled, *The Happiness of the People*. The happiness he spoke of was not something fleeting like what we might feel when our favorite team wins a big game. Murray spoke about lasting satisfaction, happiness with a deeper, transcendent meaning—human flourishing. He asserted that in the case of society and culture, there are only four things that contribute to that deep, lasting kind of happiness: family, community, vocation, and faith.

This was a remarkable moment. A secular scholar lecturing on public policy said that faith is one of the few things that is crucial to deep happiness—to human flourishing. Although that should not be news to us as Christians, it is nice to get confirmation from outside the church! Murray did not stop with that basic statement, however. In speaking about the United States, secular scholar Charles Murray said that the United States needed a Great Awakening. According to Murray, Great Awakenings are not "dispassionate, polite reconsiderations of opinions. They [are] renewals of faith, felt in the gut." [63] In his view, there was an urgent need for a Great Awakening.

Christians in the Wesleyan traditions know something about Great Awakenings. At one time in history, we specialized in them. When the Holy Spirit was unleashed in the First Great Awakening in England and America, people's lives were transformed. This was a transformation not only with future, eternal implications but also one that was experienced in the present. The Methodist movement, with its emphasis on care of the whole person—body, mind, and spirit—became a channel for human flourishing through the power of the Holy Spirit, both in the present and in the age to come.

The transformative effects of the Holy Spirit's movement during the First and Second Great Awakenings were not only individual but also societal. People boldly worked for freedom on a variety of political and social fronts. Women were empowered to assert their leadership and other gifts. Societal problems were tackled with passion and persistence. Education, health, labor—these and more were environments in which Holy Spirit boldness was brought to bear.

Transformation through the power of the Holy Spirit—on an individual and societal level—is not just possible today, it is desperately needed. Even secular scholars believe that to be true. Our world is not as God would have it be.

One of my mentors, Bishop Mvume Dandala, grew up and ministered in the Methodist Church of Southern Africa during South Africa's apartheid years and onward as the country moved toward a new future of justice and reconciliation. Years ago, I interviewed him for a podcast I hosted. He said that in South Africa, even the trees needed saving! Our world can be a dark place. A place where genocide occurs and no one notices. A place where children die because they do not have access to a 28-cent immunization and where half the world has no access to clean drinking water. A place where the pornography industry exploits women and children, and where human beings are trafficked as slaves. Violence reigns. Heartbreak is everywhere. Even the trees need saving.

> We desperately need transformation through the power of the Holy Spirit—on an individual and societal level. Our world is not as God would have it be.

Faith in Christ is a source of human flourishing through the power of the Holy Spirit. *Now.* We seem to have lost touch with that deep truth and the sense of urgency that goes with it. Though we may experience transformation in our own personal lives, we are less inclined to become channels of that same transformation in the lives of others. Though the good news *is good news*, we are afraid to share it. But God became human in Jesus to bring life, *abundant* life, to all of creation—even the trees. Salvation in Christ is whole-creation salvation where not only individuals but also systems and structures and environments and relationships are redeemed and made whole. This is not only a future reality but also one that begins now.

In a world as broken as ours, there is an urgent need for God's whole-creation salvation. Like the circular nature of embrace, as followers of Jesus, our personal transformation empowers us to become channels of Holy Spirit transformation in the lives of others. It also impels us to join God in boldly working to redeem the systems and structures that undermine human flourishing. When we become channels for God's salvation, all creation moves closer to God's intended wholeness.

How does your faith contribute to your flourishing in the present?

What aspects of your community are urgently in need of God's redemption? How might you be a channel of Holy Spirit transformation in those circumstances?

The bold urgency that is an essential value of authentic faith-sharing reflects the tension between the earthly and the eternal. There is an urgent need for us to be bold in sharing the gospel because our world needs God's redemptive grace, *now*—even the trees need saving. This is the earthly aspect of our urgency and boldness.

The eternal aspect is larger in scope but in some parts of the world is, ironically, more difficult to discuss. Eternal urgency can challenge some of us because it requires that we face the reality of sin and our separation from God. We can debate the nature of sin, but its evidence is all around us as our discussion above attests. There are numerous ways to understand sin—as woundedness, as willful disobedience, as rejection of divine initiative. Yet, however we understand it, sin separates us from God. We focus on ourselves at the expense of relationship. Our wholeness is shattered because we are captive to our own distorted vision of ourselves, others, and the world.

And yet, as we have seen, God desires to be in relationship with us and seeks us with unfailing energy and grace. God's love for us is so great that God always perseveres, continuing to pursue us and reach out to us. God never gives up.

Our Triune God is like a celestial GPS. When we take a wrong turn, God finds a new way. The Holy Spirit may warn us to make a U-turn; however, if there is no U-turn, God recalculates our route and the Holy Spirit nudges us in a new direction. God would rather redirect us than abandon us. Yet we remain in the driver's seat. Because God respects our freedom—our sacred right of acceptance or refusal—God will never force or manipulate us. We drive the car. This freedom is a tremendous gift. It is also the source of our urgency.

Each human being is free to accept God's offer of forgiveness, mercy, and grace, which leads to eternal life. When we turn away from sin and toward God, we anticipate the resurrection of our bodies and life everlasting in God's New Creation. Each human being is also free to reject God's offer of forgiveness, mercy, and grace. The results of that choice are more difficult to contemplate, because that choice brings us face to face with the issue of judgment and the possibility of eternal separation from God.

"This is how much God loved the world: He gave his Son, his one and only Son. And this is why: so that no one need be destroyed; by believing in him, anyone can have a whole and lasting life. God didn't go to all the trouble of sending his Son merely to point an accusing finger, telling the world how bad it was. He came to help, to put the world right again"

(John 3:16-17 MSG).

The issue is complicated by the difficulty of separating human judgment from God's judgment. Like much of Christian faith, there is mystery here. God alone is the authority in the divine-human relationship. It is not for us to judge who is in right relationship with God and who is not. That truth lies at the heart of embrace. We open our arms before all else—before judgment, before confession, before redemption.

It is beyond our ability to comprehend the ways of God and the extent to which God would go to be in a relationship of love and wholeness with us. If the crucifixion of Jesus is any indication, God will go to unfathomable lengths. Even so, the possibility of being separated from God is no small thing. We are not the judges of another person's salvation; that responsibility belongs to God alone. However, that does not mean an urgent need for others to experience the life-transforming grace of God in Jesus Christ does not still exist. If our love for others is genuine, contemplating the prospect of their eternal separation from God should energize us to show and share the love of Jesus, not out of a fear of their judgment but out of a desire for them to experience true life here and now—and for all eternity.

As an English-only speaker, I am often envious of other languages that can sum up, in one word, concepts that in English take entire sentences to explain. There are wonderful words in many different languages that point to a depth of meaning that far outweighs a single word. The German word *mutterseelenallein* is such a word. *Mutterseelenallein* began as a French phrase: *moi tout seul*. It was used in the eighteenth century by the Huguenots, a group of persecuted French Protestants who fled to Germany. The Huguenots used this phrase to describe their feeling of isolation and dislocation from home. Apparently, the Germans misunderstood the phrase, thinking it was *mutterseelen*, which means "mother souls." However, the phrase did not make sense to them, so they added the word *allein*, which means "alone." [64]

Mutterseelenallein: to be so utterly and extremely alone and lonely that no one could even find you or reach for you—physically, mentally, and spiritually

When you are *mutterseelenallein*, you are all alone—literally "mother souls alone." There are no souls around you, not even your mother. To be *mutterseelenallein* is not simply to be alone, but to be utterly, completely alone. Abandoned, isolated. It is to be so alone and lonely that no one could ever find you or reach for you—physically, mentally, spiritually.

God does not desire any of God's creatures to be *mutterseelenallein*. And yet God loves us so much that rather than forcing us to be in relationship, God is willing to risk that we will choose to be just that, *mutterseelenallein*, so utterly and completely alone that no one can ever find us or reach us. The thought of that possibility should fill us with both a bold urgency and an urgent boldness.

How have you experienced the eternal urgency of the gospel in your own walk of faith?

How has a sense of eternal urgency affected your approach to sharing your faith? How might you look at faith-sharing differently if you were to grasp more deeply the urgent nature of the gospel?

CONCLUDING THOUGHTS

Showing and sharing the love of Jesus from a stance of embrace is not a strategy. It is the core of God's kingdom agenda. Because it is the way in which God relates to all of creation, it is the way we relate to the world as we seek to make the gospel known. Embrace models God's activity in the world and makes itself available as a channel of that activity. Thus, in opening our arms and creating space within ourselves for others, space is also created for the working of the Holy Spirit. And then, while we wait, God works.

When we lay hold of the essential values that ground authentic faith-sharing, we are empowered to make known that the gospel of Jesus the Messiah is good news for all creation. As we embody embrace, we work and wait with expectant hope that those outside the church will come to know a God who is steadfast and faithful in keeping God's promises. That they will discover a God who desires that no one be left out of the one family of Abraham. A God who shares with humanity all that it means to be human. That they will experience a God who is present through the Spirit within and among believers, going before them into the world and working through them for redemption. A God who is working, even now, to eliminate evil and bring to fruition the justice and peace of the kingdom begun in Jesus of Nazareth.

As we embody embrace, we work and wait with expectant hope that those outside the church will come to understand the good news for their future. That they will encounter the hope of eternal life: first in the presence of Christ as he is now seated at the right hand of God. And finally in resurrected bodies when he returns to establish God's kingdom in a world transformed and remade into New Creation—a world where all of creation is redeemed and restored to its intended wholeness.

The essential values of evangelism rooted in embrace point to the truth that the gospel is not a message to be privatized. It has been entrusted to the body of Christ. We make it known to the world through our communal life when we embody Jesus' expansive welcome and invitation. When we live in solidarity with the poor and suffering. When the presence of the Holy Spirit of Jesus can be met and experienced in our worshiping life together. We make it known through the sharing of our own stories, our commitment to prayer, and our willingness to live as witnesses to the faithfulness of Jesus through our own faithful obedience to the God who sent him.

The gospel is good news for all creation. When we commit ourselves to showing and sharing the love of Jesus, we are *sharing and demonstrating* that Jesus is the renewer of the *whole* creation, the *entire* face of the earth, *all* the dimensions of life. As Christians, the salvation we proclaim is that big. The news is that good.

PRAY ABOUT IT

As you begin your time of prayer, review the list of names you created during the study, the needs you were going to pray about, and the ways in which you planned to enter these persons' lives. With a new sense of urgency, bring these names and needs before God and open yourself to the next steps God may have for these relationships.

ACT ON IT

Using the list created during this study, and insights gained from prayer, outline a plan for deepening these relationships and beginning the ongoing process of embrace.

GROUP MEETING ~ **SESSION SIX**

THIS IS YOUR final time together in this study. If members plan to stay together for a longer period, finalize your plans. World Methodist Evangelism provides training for those interested in further study or in teaching on behalf of WME across the Wesleyan family in all parts of the world. Visit www.world-methodist.org/embrace for additional information or contact info@worldmethodist.org.

OPENING PRAYER

INSIGHTS AND CHALLENGES

Review the notes you made of your reflections during the week.

What new insight did you gain?

What challenge did you encounter?

Invite each person to share an insight and a challenge encountered in the material.

SHARING TOGETHER

1. Discuss the contrast between lament and celebration in response to the fact that one-third of the world is Christian. What does that say about our current age?

2. Share initial reactions to the idea of earthly urgency. How does this concept resonate?

3. Invite group members to share how their faith contributes to their experience of human flourishing.

4. Discuss areas that people identified in your community that are urgently in need of God's redemption and the ways persons might become channels of Holy Spirit transformation. Are there additional ways that your church or a smaller group might embody embrace in these circumstances?

5. Spend some time reflecting on how a sense of eternal urgency affects our approach to sharing faith. What might group members or churches do differently considering the urgent nature of the gospel?

6. Spend the remainder of your time discussing ways your group might continue to pray for and act in the lives of the persons named on the index cards that have been shared throughout the study. How might you implement what you have learned? What next step do you need to take as individuals or as a group to continue the ongoing nature of embrace?

ACT ON IT

Decide on a concrete plan based on your discussion in number 6.

PRAY ABOUT IT

Spend some time in prayer over your ongoing plan to embody embrace in the aftermath of this study. Invite members of the group to pray aloud as they feel led. Close your time of prayer by once again praying aloud the Prayer of St. Francis:

Lord, make me an instrument of your peace;
  where there is hatred, let me sow love;
  where there is injury, pardon;
  where there is doubt, faith;
  where there is despair, hope;
  where there is darkness, light;
  and where there is sadness, joy.
O Divine Master, grant that I may not so much seek
  to be consoled as to console;
  to be understood as to understand;
  to be loved as to love;
  for it is in giving that we receive;
  it is in pardoning that we are pardoned;
  and it is in dying that we are born to eternal life. Amen.

ENDNOTES

1 I am indebted to my friend Ed Stetzer for introducing me to the phrase "showing and sharing the love of Jesus" as a way to describe evangelism.

2 Miroslav Volf, *Exclusion and Embrace: A Theological Exploration of Identity, Otherness, and Reconciliation* (Nashville: Abingdon Press, 1996).

3 H. Eddie Fox and George E. Morris, *Faith-Sharing: Dynamic Christian Witnessing by Invitation* (Nashville: Discipleship Resources, 1996).

4 Kenneth J. Collins, *The Theology of John Wesley: Holy Love and the Shape of Grace* (Nashville: Abingdon Press, 2007), 21.

5 Jürgen Moltmann, *The Spirit of Life: A Universal Affirmation* [1992], trans. M. Kohl (Minneapolis: Fortress Press, 2001), 129-138.

6 Volf, *Exclusion and Embrace*, 127-128.

7 Luke Timothy Johnson, *The Real Jesus: The Misguided Quest for the Historical Jesus and the Truth of the Traditional Gospels* (New York: HarperOne, 1996), 158.

8 Collins, *Theology*, 13-14, 23-24.

9 Kirsteen Kim, *The Holy Spirit in the World: A Global Conversation* (Maryknoll: Orbis Books, 2007), 15-19.

10 Volf, *Exclusion and Embrace*, 141.

11 Volf, *Exclusion and Embrace*, 143 (emphasis original).

12 Vincent J. Donovan, *Christianity Rediscovered* (Maryknoll: Orbis Books, 1978), 48.

13 Volf, *Exclusion and Embrace*, 65-66 (emphasis added).

14 Cornelius Plantinga, Jr., *Not the Way It's Supposed to Be: A Breviary of Sin* (Grand Rapids: William B. Eerdmans, 1995), 30.

15 N. T. Wright, *Justification: God's Plan and Paul's Vision* (Downers Grove, IL: IVP Academic, 2009), 55-77.

16 James D. G. Dunn, *Jesus Remembered*, vol. 1, *Christianity in the Making* (Grand Rapids: William B. Eerdmans, 2003), 528-532, 605-607.

17 Volf, *Exclusion and Embrace*, 141-142. (Volf provides an extended description of the four messages conveyed by opening our arms.)

18 H. Eddie Fox and George E. Morris, "The Basics of Christian Conversion and Discipleship," *The Faith-Sharing New Testament with Psalms* (Nashville: Cokesbury, 2010), ix. Fox and Morris provide a discussion of the components of this definition in *Faith-Sharing: Dynamic Christian Witnessing by Invitation* (Nashville: Discipleship Resources, 1996) 33-37.

19 Fox and Morris, *Faith-Sharing*, 33.

20 Fox and Morris, *Faith-Sharing*, 34.

21 Fox and Morris, *Faith-Sharing*, 34-35.

22 Howard A. Snyder and Joel Scandrett, *Salvation Means Creation Healed: The Ecology of Sin and Grace: Overcoming the Divorce between Earth and Heaven* (Eugene, OR: Cascade Books, 2011) 68.

23 Lexilogos.com (William Whittaker, Latin-English Dictionary, University of Notre Dame, 2010) http://archives.nd.edu/cgi-bin/wordz.pl?english=salvation (accessed 3/23/2017).

24 Fox and Morris, *Faith-Sharing*, 35.

25 Wright, *Justification*, 99.

26 Fox and Morris, *Faith-Sharing*, 36.

27 Snyder and Scandrett, *Salvation Means Creation Healed*, 94.

28 Jason E. Vickers, "Wesley's Theological Emphases," *The Cambridge Companion to John Wesley*, Randy L. Maddox and Jason E. Vickers, eds. (New York: Cambridge University Press, 2010), 201.

29 John Wesley, Sermon 7, "The Way to the Kingdom," *John Wesley's Sermons: An Anthology*, Albert C. Outler and Richard P. Heitzenrater, eds. (Nashville: Abingdon, 1991), 124-132.

30 Fox and Morris, *Faith-Sharing*, 36.

31 Volf, *Exclusion and Embrace*, 142-143. (Volf provides a helpful discussion of the importance of waiting.)

32 Maxie Dunnam, *The Workbook of Intercessory Prayer* (Nashville: Upper Room Books, 1979), 25.

33 Dunnam, *Intercessory Prayer*, 25.

34 Dunnam, *Intercessory Prayer*, 25.

35 Dunnam, *Intercessory Prayer*, 41.

36 Dunnam, *Intercessory Prayer*, 71.

37 Dunnam, *Intercessory Prayer*, 73-74, 76.

38 Dunnam, *Intercessory Prayer*, 80.

39 Dunnam, *Intercessory Prayer*, 81.

40 https://www.merriam-webster.com/dictionary/integrity

41 Volf, *Exclusion and Embrace*, 143-144. (Volf provides a detailed description of this element of embrace.)

42 Volf, *Exclusion and Embrace*, 143 (emphasis original).

43 Fox and Morris, *Faith-Sharing*, 53.

44 Fox and Morris, *The Faith-Sharing New Testament*, ix.

45 H. Eddie Fox and George E. Morris, "The Basics of Christian Conversion and Discipleship," *The Faith-Sharing New Testament with Psalms* (Nashville: Cokesbury, 2010), ix.

46 Fox and Morris, *Faith-Sharing*, 55, Cf. George E. Morris, *The Mystery and Meaning of Christian Conversion* (Nashville: Discipleship Resources, 1981).

47 Fox and Morris, *Faith-Sharing*, 55.

48 Fox and Morris, *Faith-Sharing*, 56

49 Fox and Morris, *Faith-Sharing*, 105.

50 Fox and Morris, *Faith-Sharing*, 104.

51 Fox and Morris, *Faith-Sharing*, 95.

52 Fox and Morris, *Faith-Sharing*, 72.

53 Fox and Morris, *Faith-Sharing*, 73.

54 Jürgen Moltmann, *The Way of Jesus Christ: Christology in Messianic Dimensions* [1989], trans. M. Kohl (Minneapolis: Fortress Press, 1993), 45.

55 Fox and Morris, *Faith-Sharing*, 57.

56 Everett F. Harrison, "Romans," *Expositor's Bible Commentary*, Frank E. Gaebelein, ed. (Grand Rapids: Zondervan, 1976), 156.

57 Volf, *Exclusion and Embrace*, 144-145. (Volf provides a helpful description of this last stage of embrace.)

58 Volf, *Exclusion and Embrace*, 71.

59 Kim, *Holy Spirit*, 150.

60 James D. G. Dunn, *The Christ and the Spirit: Pneumatology*, vol. 2 (Grand Rapids: William B. Eerdmans, 1998), 68.

61 James K. A. Smith, "Thinking in Tongues," *First Things* 182 (April, 2008) http://www.firstthings.com/print.php ?type=article&year=2008&month=03&title_link=00 3-thinking-in-tongues-36 (6 June 2009).

62 Kim, *Holy Spirit*, 152.

63 Charles Murray, "The Happiness of the People," *Irving Krystol Lecture*, The American Enterprise Institute, 2009, https://www.aei.org/research-products/speech/the-happiness-of-the-people (March 25, 2021).

64 Anne-Sophie Brandlin, *DW: Made for Minds*, "Word of the Week: Mutterseelenallein," March 28, 2014, http://www.dw.com/en/mutterseelenallein/a-17527665 (February 17, 2017).

CPSIA information can be obtained
at www.ICGtesting.com
Printed in the USA
LVHW100032020921
696732LV00003B/3